Healthy Ageing after COVID-19

Written by researchers and experienced health professionals from Hong Kong, China, Chiu and Law identify and examine important issues of healthy ageing after COVID-19 from research and policy perspectives in the Asian contexts. This book opens with discussions of healthy ageing from personal, social, economic, and political perspectives. These discussions make reference to the key characteristics of a community health model. It aims to examine the impacts of the COVID-19 pandemic on aged care in an international perspective, citing the fifth wave of COVID-19 in Hong Kong as a case report. Comprehensive analysis on the influence of COVID-19 infection on Hong Kong and the implemented anti-pandemic policy measures, as well as recommendations of post-pandemic policies to promote healthy ageing, are provided. This monograph also reviews the worldwide impacts on aged care during and after the pandemic, as well as the experience of aged care services in Hong Kong and other Asia-Pacific regions. The responding changes in policies and strategies for healthy ageing in selected countries are also reviewed. This monograph ends with a highlight on the design and development of a community model for healthy ageing, providing insights to the achievement of sustainable healthy ageing with reference to the sustainable development goal (SDG) 3.

A valuable resource to governments, politicians, academics, and practitioners, it is intended for formulating future directions of relevant research, and the design and implementation of interventions for the promotion of healthy ageing in the post-pandemic era.

Wang-Kin Chiu is Senior Lecturer at the College of Professional and Continuing Education (CPCE) of The Hong Kong Polytechnic University (PolyU). He is Management Committee Member of the Centre for Ageing and Healthcare Management Research (CAHMR) of CPCE at PolyU.

Vincent T. S. Law is Senior Lecturer at the College of Professional and Continuing Education (CPCE) of The Hong Kong Polytechnic University (PolyU). He is also the Founding Member and Deputy Director of the Centre for Ageing and Healthcare Management Research (CAHMR) of PolyU CPCE.

Routledge Focus on Business and Management

The fields of business and management have grown exponentially as areas of research and education. This growth presents challenges for readers trying to keep up with the latest important insights. *Routledge Focus on Business and Management* presents small books on big topics and how they intersect with the world of business research.

Individually, each title in the series provides coverage of a key academic topic, whilst collectively, the series forms a comprehensive collection across the business disciplines.

Knowledge Management and AI in Society 5.0
Manlio Del Giudice, Veronica Scuotto and Armando Papa

The Logistics Audit
Methods, Organization and Practice
Piotr Buła and Bartosz Niedzielski

Women's Social Entrepreneurship
Case Studies from the United Kingdom
Panagiotis Kyriakopoulos

Business Schools post-Covid-19
A Blueprint for Survival
Andreas Kaplan

Sustainable Governance in B Corps
Non-Financial Reporting for Sustainable Development
Patrizia Gazzola and Matteo Ferioli

Happiness and Wellbeing in Singapore
Beyond Economic Prosperity
Siok Kuan Tambyah, Tan Soo Jiuan and Yuen Wei Lun

Healthy Ageing after COVID-19
Research and Policy Perspectives from Asia
Edited by Wang-Kin Chiu and Vincent T.S. Law

For more information about this series, please visit: www.routledge.com/Routledge
-Focus-on-Business-and-Management/book-series/FBM

Healthy Ageing after COVID-19

Research and Policy Perspectives from Asia

Edited by Wang-Kin Chiu and Vincent T. S. Law

LONDON AND NEW YORK

First published 2024
by Routledge
4 Park Square, Milton Park, Abingdon, Oxon OX14 4RN

and by Routledge
605 Third Avenue, New York, NY 10158

Routledge is an imprint of the Taylor & Francis Group, an informa business

© 2024 selection and editorial matter, Wang-Kin Chiu and Vincent T. S. Law; individual chapters, the contributors

The right of Wang-Kin Chiu and Vincent T. S. Law to be identified as the authors of the editorial material, and of the authors for their individual chapters, has been asserted in accordance with sections 77 and 78 of the Copyright, Designs and Patents Act 1988.

British Library Cataloguing-in-Publication Data
A catalogue record for this book is available from the British Library

Library of Congress Cataloging-in-Publication Data
Names: Chiu, Wang-Kin, editor. | Law, Vincent Tin Sing, editor.
Title: Healthy ageing after COVID-19: research and policy perspectives from Asia / edited by Wang-Kin Chiu and Vincent T.S. Law.
Description: Abingdon, Oxon; New York, NY: Routledge, 2024. | Series: Routledge focus on business and management | Includes bibliographical references.
Identifiers: LCCN 2023055940 (print) | LCCN 2023055941 (ebook) | ISBN 9781032567181 (hardback) | ISBN 9781032567211 (paperback) | ISBN 9781003436881 (ebook)
Subjects: LCSH: Older people–Care–Asia. | Older people–Government policy–Asia. | Aging–Health aspects–Asia. | COVID-19 Pandemic, 2020–Influence.
Classification: LCC HV1484.A78 H435 2024 (print) | LCC HV1484.A78 (ebook) | DDC 362.6095–dc23/eng/20240117
LC record available at https://lccn.loc.gov/2023055940
LC ebook record available at https://lccn.loc.gov/2023055941

ISBN: 978-1-032-56718-1 (hbk)
ISBN: 978-1-032-56721-1 (pbk)
ISBN: 978-1-003-43688-1 (ebk)

DOI: 10.4324/9781003436881

Typeset in Times New Roman
by Deanta Global Publishing Services, Chennai, India

Contents

Figure

Table

List of Contributors

List of Contributors

Ms Yumi Y. T. Chan
Dr Wang-Kin Chiu
Dr Ben Y. F. Fong
Ms Carina Y. H. Lam
Dr Vincent T. S. Law
Mr Tommy K. C. Ng

Biographies of Authors (for reference if necessary, extracted from proposal)

Ms Yumi Y. T. Chan is a Fellow of the Hong Kong College of Community Health Practitioners. She obtained BSc (Hons) in Applied Sciences (Health Studies), and the Master of Nutrition and Healthy Ageing programme at PolyU. She has been an Intern at the Centre for Ageing and Healthcare Management Research at the School of Professional Education and Executive Development (SPEED) of The Hong Kong Polytechnic University (PolyU). She studied health-related subjects and had participated in a community-based service-learning project to promote healthy lifestyle to older residents. She had acquired health-related information when joining field placements in Hong Kong Community College (HKCC) of PolyU. She actively seeks to meet people who inspire her in the health care sector and put massive effort and commitment to health promotion in the community.

Dr Wang-Kin Chiu received his Bachelor of Science (first class honours) and PhD in Chemistry from The Chinese University of Hong Kong. He is a Senior Lecturer at the College of Professional and Continuing Education (CPCE) of The Hong Kong Polytechnic University (PolyU). He is currently serving as the Assistant Programme Leader of Associate in Health Studies and the Assistant Award Leader of Bachelor of Science (Honours) in Applied Sciences (Health Studies). Dr Chiu is also a

Management Committee Member of the Centre for Ageing and Healthcare Management Research (CAHMR) of CPCE at PolyU. He has published journal papers and book chapters related to ageing population and sustainable environment.

Dr Ben Y. F. Fong graduated in Medicine from the University of Sydney, where he also obtained his Master's degree in public health. He had his clinical training in Sydney and has held senior management position at Prince Henry Hospital, a teaching hospital. He is a Specialist in Community Medicine, holding Honorary Clinical Associate Professorship at the two local medical schools in Hong Kong. He is currently the Professor of Practice (Health Studies) and Associate Division Head of the Division of Science, Engineering and Health Studies, and Centre Director of the Centre for Ageing and Healthcare Management Research, of the College of Professional and Continuing Education, The Hong Kong Polytechnic University. He is also Adjunct Professor in Public Health & Tropical Medicine in the College of Public Health, Medical and Veterinary Sciences at James Cook University, Queensland, Australia. He has contributed to publications as lead editor of three books in English, including recent titles of *"Routledge Handbook of Public Health and the Community"* in 2021 and *"Primary Care Revisited - Interdisciplinary Perspectives for a New Era"* in 2020, over 30 health books in Chinese, and 50 journal papers.

Ms Carina Y. H. Lam is a Fellow of the Hong Kong College of Community Health Practitioners. She is an Enrolled Nurse (General) registered with The Nursing Council of Hong Kong with working experience in the nursing homes. She has obtained her bachelor's degree in Health Studies from the School of Professional Education and Executive Development (SPEED) of The Hong Kong Polytechnic University (PolyU), and the Master of Nutrition and Healthy Ageing programme at PolyU. She is also a nurse of Olive Nursing Home, an intern of the Centre for Ageing and Healthcare Management Research of PolyU SPEED, an Associate Fellow of the Hong Kong College of Community Health Practitioners, and an intern of the Family Planning Association of Hong Kong, where she is the chairman of the Sexuality Education Youth Volunteer Team.

Dr Vincent T. S. Law is a Senior Lecturer of the College of Professional and Continuing Education (CPCE) of The Hong Kong Polytechnic University (PolyU). He is currently the Scheme Leader of the Bachelor of Social Sciences (Honours) Scheme. Vincent is also the Founding Member and Deputy Director of the Centre for Ageing and Healthcare Management Research (CAHMR) of PolyU CPCE. Being an experienced researcher in public policy, Vincent participated in some large-scale consultancy or research projects on public policy and public engagement with the Hong Kong government in recent years. He authored a few academic journal papers, edited three books on healthcare, authored some book chapters on healthcare and sustainability, and published five Chinese books on Chinese philosophy.

Dr Chor-ming Lum received his bachelor's degree in Medicine and Surgery from The University of Hong Kong and his master's degree in Public Health from The Chinese University of Hong Kong. He is also a Fellow of Hong Kong Academy of Medicine, Royal College of Physicians of Australasia, Royal College of Physicians of Edinburgh and Royal College of Physicians and Surgeons of Glasgow. Currently, Dr Lum is Consultant at Department of Medicine and Geriatrics, Kowloon West Cluster of the Hong Kong Hospital Authority and Consultant for End of Life Care Project at Institute of Ageing, Chinese University of Hong Kong, Co-Director of the Master in Clinical Gerontology and End of Life Care program at Chinese University of Hong Kong. He is also Honorary teaching staff at Department of Medicine and Department of Family Medicine / Primary Care at both University of Hong Kong and Chinese University of Hong Kong. Dr Lum has extensive experience in training specialist in Geriatric Medicine, specialist in Family Medicine on care of older adults, and promotion of healthy ageing at community level to different healthcare professionals and laypersons.

Mr Tommy K. C. Ng is the Project Associate in the Centre for Ageing and Healthcare Management Research (CAHMR) of PolyU CPCE. In this position at CAHMR, he is actively involved in research related to health topics and is responsible for organising different research activities, including conferences, research seminars and methodology workshops. He has recently published research papers in international journals. His research interests include primary care and public health.

1 Healthy ageing in the personal, social, economic, and political perspectives

Ben Y. F. Fong and Wang-Kin Chiu

Abstract

The growing ageing population in the developed economies is the result of longer life expectancy and low mortality rates, which have contributed to a hitherto unprecedented population-ageing phenomenon. Healthy ageing echoes the definition of 'health' as including not only physical and mental health, but also social well-being by the World Health Organization (WHO). Ageing is viewed as a positive process which is full of opportunities and needs. The promotion and maintenance of good health among our older population presents a special challenge not only to older persons themselves but also to the political, social, and health leaders. It is a concern beyond the current generation of older population, and perhaps the entire population. To achieve healthy or successful ageing, absence of disease, absence of disability, preserved cognitive performance, appropriate physical performance, optimal intrinsic capacity, and active social participation are the key and indispensable factors for individual older adults. Governments need to enhance multisectoral collaboration and transdisciplinary consultations in policy development and strengthen the building blocks of the health system, to formulate and implement the national work plan for an integrated healthcare model designed for healthy ageing. This chapter will discuss healthy ageing in the personal, social, economic, and political perspectives.

Life expectancy

The world has been witnessing an increasingly growing ageing population in the last decade in the more developed economies since World War II. The trend has arisen from the prolonged life expectancy which is due to the interconnected improvement in economy, education, technology, nutrition, environment, and medical care, and the low mortality rates, associated with improved economy, cumulative personal wealth, better living conditions, safe environment, adequate food supply, advancement in medicine and technology, better understanding of diseases, and availability of health services with qualified healthcare professionals, research and modern medicine, public

DOI: 10.4324/9781003436881-1

health, primary and long-term care, public awareness, community engagement, and disaster management (Chung & Marmot, 2020). More people are living in planned and built-up cities and townships where housing is constructed for comfort, convenience, and safety. However, with the extended lifespan and modern facilities, city dwellers are not necessarily healthier as the air is polluted by exhaust fumes from motor vehicles and industrial processes, the environment and water are potentially contaminated by heavy metals and industrial wastes, and mental well-being is grossly affected by crowded living and stressful lifestyles.

Hong Kong has had the longest life expectancy for over a decade and this is against all odds. The city is small, crowded, busy, and virtually functions non-stop around the clock. Life is stressful. Long working hours are the norm. People strive to live better but properties are so precious. Residents either join the long queue for public housing or work their guts out to own an "undersized" flat. However, people are fairly happy and most enjoy social activities, particularly eating out with family, friends, colleagues, and mates. Choices of food are abundant in this little Asia's World City of multicultural and subcultural communities. The commonly cited factors for long life expectancy in Hong Kong are the universally accessible and affordable healthcare services in the public sector, heavily subsidised by the government. At the same time, people have free choices in the private services and those available in the Greater Bay Area, comprising nine municipalities in the Guangdong Province plus two Special Administrative Regions of Hong Kong and Macao. In addition, ambulance service is fully operated by the government and ambulances arrive at the destination within 12 minutes in response to emergency calls. Another reason for the long life expectancy is the genetic pool and mix. As observed by the author, the vast majority of residents have their ancestry from all parts of China. There have been a number of major migrations to Hong Kong in the last century. Individuals have parents and grandparents who originally came from distant clans.

Longevity is regarded as a blessing in all cultures, but living a long life may not be a good thing for some individuals if there is no quality of life, or if one is home-bound or even bed-bound. Everyone must have lived, and most have worked, for several decades before getting old. What does it mean to be old? This is a very simple question to answer—ageing implies getting towards the end or final stage of life or presence on earth as a living creature. The world has witnessed the longest and worst-ever pandemic for the last three to four years since the beginning of 2020 with the novel infectious disease, COVID-19. All the countries and regions have been gradually recovering from the plunging economy, social disorientation, and massive loss of lives and opportunities. The older adults have suffered seriously and many of them have passed away because of their vulnerable bodies, or lack of care or vaccination. Hence, aligning health systems to the needs of older adults, whether during public health emergencies or other times, should be one of the priorities in building a healthy ageing population.

This monograph aims to examine the impacts of the COVID-19 pandemic on aged care from an international perspective, citing the fifth wave of COVID-19 pandemic in Hong Kong, China, during early 2022 as a case report. The responding changes in policies and strategies for healthy ageing in selected countries or regions are also reviewed. Research on community models for sustainable healthy ageing is also reviewed to provide insights for governments, politicians, academics, and practitioners.

Ageing

Biologically, all cells, organs, and body systems have life cycles in which they grow, develop, mature, age, and eventually die. Strictly speaking, ageing begins when a life is born, but this process of change becomes apparent and more noticeable after the full development and maturity of the body. There are periods of rapid growth and development from birth, infancy, childhood, to adolescence, and the subsequent natural changes in physiological functions throughout adulthood. The associated biological and psychological states vary as a person grows older year after year in the life course. The more visible milestones of lifelong ageing are the bodily feelings characterised by symptoms of mid-life 'crisis' and menopause, followed by old age.

Biological ageing often leads to deterioration in eyesight, such as presbyopia, cataracts, and macular degeneration, impaired hearing, dental conditions, and greying of hair, with various degrees of damage. The extent and speed of decline depend on the care and attention of individuals towards their body and maintenance of health, and the subsequent adaptive capacities and coping skills to achieve optimum well-being when the symptoms appear. Some older adults are tough people in this regard.

Personality and mental functions change throughout life from the continuous process of psychosocial interaction in daily living, work, education, and community activities, representing psychological growth, development, and adaptation of individuals. Psychological ageing involves learning and corresponding reactions to psychosocial events, including stress and life crisis. Such lifelong experience is accumulated from exposure to different events as a person goes through different stages of life. Decline in intelligence, learning abilities, and memory are expected among older adults, although they are often considered as wise mentors because of their age and seniority. Unfortunately, older adults often suffer from mental conditions, particularly depression, and have a higher suicide rate. Hence, maintaining psychosocial well-being, especially after retirement, should be a top priority in aged care for the older adults themselves, their family and carers, and healthcare providers. They must continue to be active and enjoy life. There is a Chinese saying of 'do not get terribly bad at the end (of life)'.

Clinically, geriatric syndromes describe some common complex health states seen in ageing. They are caused by a number of possibly concurrent abnormal bodily conditions like frailty, urinary incontinence, mental impairment, and pressure ulcers. Frailty is noted to be an emerging health burden in the world, arising from continuing changes and minor decline in the immune, musculoskeletal, and endocrine systems of older adults, associated with fatigue, decreased muscle strength, and an increase in falls and mortality. The affected older adults appear to shrink, feel weak and exhausted, and move slowly, resulting in low activity, cognitive impairment, and poor balance, but they may maintain almost full daily life capacity (Fong, 2022). Risk factors of frailty include multi-morbidity, polypharmacy, female gender, low socioeconomic status and educational background, poor diet, and physical inactivity. There is a potential for severe long-term effects on the well-being of the affected older adults who are less ready or able to recover from illnesses or injuries. This can have a real impact on the quality of daily living and life expectancy.

Nonetheless, old age is not necessarily associated with poor health and disability. In fact, the health status of older persons of comparable age-cohorts in some overseas countries has continued to improve during the last century. Ageing is essentially the intervened outcome of successful public health and social policies in combating diseases, accidents, and injuries, supported by socioeconomic development and medical advancements (World Health Organization, 2020; Lu et al., 2021). Ageing must be regarded as a natural process and should be taken as a positive process in which there are opportunities for personal development and social contributions as long as one lives in the world. Apart from health and mental needs, there are also needs for family support and psychosocial care, friends and social connectivity, finance, housing, activities of daily living, continuing education and lifelong learning, retirement protection, new skills, rehabilitation, etc.

The challenges of ageing

The promotion and maintenance of good health and well-being among older adults is a real and very demanding challenge to older persons and their family and carers. It is also a social, academic, financial, and political challenge to the government, health and social care professionals, university researchers, non-governmental organisations (NGOs), private companies, politicians, and local communities. In fact, such challenges are also encountered and dealt with by the younger generation, who will become old one day themselves, though they are acting as the family, children, and perhaps carers for the current generation of the older population. Overall, the challenges affect the entire population, which is ageing more than before in history as life expectancy is getting longer. These impacts are affecting most countries which are also facing the adverse socioeconomic effects of shrinking working populations.

Issues of sustainability and equity related to ageing are on the national agenda of many governments.

Challenges for older adults

While older adults are seen to be well-positioned to face the challenges of life with the experience accumulated over the decades in the life course, many of them are potentially vulnerable in dealing with and managing changes arising from ageing. There is a lot to learn, cope with, and compromise when starting to live the 'new' life characterised by changes from ageing when a person becomes old and frail, decline in bodily functioning, slow in responses, etc. Furthermore, older adults also have to face challenges from frequent falls, dementia, safety at home and outside, being home-bound, being bed-bound, dependency, abuse, long-term care and medicines, personality conflicts, family tides, lifelong habits, empty nest, loss of spouse, partner, or family members, social isolation, retirement adjustment, migration, second career, new family, fewer children, and so on. Therefore, individuals must be well-prepared for ageing.

Chronic degenerative conditions are essentially natural outcomes from ageing of physiological functions and biochemical processes in the human body, but they also represent the cumulative effects of individual's ways of living and the environmental impact. Older adults have to adjust to the management of such conditions for the rest of their lives. They need to take medicines daily, consult the doctors regularly for follow-up and monitoring, and be concerned about the possibility of complications and other ailments. All these management tasks may cause inconvenience in daily living and may lead to stress, and even depression, for the older adults, who may feel incapacitated because complications from chronic degenerative conditions, such as strokes and organ failure, may result in permanent disabilities. They are also prone to accidents and injuries from these conditions. Equally, mental wellness among the older adults is a major social and public health issue, and is associated with high suicide rates among the older adults, particularly in developed communities. Older adults may feel lonely, particularly if they live alone or do not have regular social activities. They may be disturbed by the adverse bodily conditions from ageing.

Challenges to the family and carers

The need for support and care from family members and carers is obvious when one gets old. Older adults require assistance in their daily living and some specific activities like medical and hospital attendance, whether they live alone or with the family. Even for those staying in residential homes for the older adults, family members are expected to visit and to volunteer some help to the older adults. Such intergenerational support and attention are embedded in the culture of most Asian societies and may also come from relatives and even neighbours. Older adults require attention in daily living routines, diet, nutrition, home safety, etc.

The challenges lie in the fact that the support and care, usually very demanding as a rule, do not commonly involve reward and there is often no predictable timeframe. The family members and carers have to be very tolerant and flexible in caring for the older adults who are physically, mentally, and even financially dependent to a great extents. The carers, too, have routine work and personal worries themselves, thus making it stressful to take care of older members of the family. Therefore, family members and carers have to understand the changes arising from ageing and the specific needs in the long-term care of senior members, who should be empowered to cope with the changes and demands of ageing and to modify their lifestyle to live comfortably and happily in their remaining years.

Challenges may also arise when making decisions on personal and family matters. Good family dynamics with close cohesiveness among members, and adequate and continuing emotional support to the older adults by family members and carers are a big help. It is always in the best interest of family members to love each other and live happily under the same roof when a family is born or formed. These challenges are more difficult to manage in single-child families, nuclear families, poor families, and disharmonious families, as well as when children are living elsewhere in other countries or regions.

Challenges for health and social care professionals

Direct challenges to the health and social care professionals from the ageing population demand continuing responses and ongoing activities from service providers involved in aged care. The professionals must be appropriately educated and trained to be competent in taking care of the older adults and in managing the changes from ageing for the latter to live an acceptable 'normal' life with quality and dignity, in close collaboration with family members and carers. It should be a holistic and integrated approach in aged care, attending to physical and psychosocial needs, involving transdisciplinary providers. Ideally, the case manager is designated to be the contact person in looking after an individual older adult, acting as the coordinator and personal advisor.

Health and social care professionals, and their academic counterparts, are in the best position to promote healthy ageing because they are trustworthy advisors for older adults and policymakers as professional advocates. The professional care providers make changes through the influence on the older adults in their behaviour, health literacy, and lifestyle to enhance them to live a better late life. Personal empowerment and encouragement are essential drivers. However, older adults and their families have expectations on the servicing professionals, well beyond health-related issues. To do a good job, a caring personality, empathy, and social skills are the key, as well as experience and knowledge.

Healthy ageing in the personal perspective

To be happy and healthy during old age, ideally, one wishes to be in a state free of diseases or chronic conditions, absence of disability or physical impairment, preserved cognitive faculty and performance, appropriate and acceptable physical performance, optimal intrinsic capacity, and active social connectivity and participation (Leung et al., 2022). Healthy ageing echoes the definition of 'health' by the World Health Organization (WHO) as including not only physical and mental health, but also social well-being. The term is used interchangeably with terms such as 'active', 'successful', or 'productive' ageing. Healthy ageing is the positive and natural process of optimising opportunities for health, building on social participation and personal security to enhance quality of life as individuals age (World Health Organization, 2020; Lu et al., 2021). Education is known to be a universally indicative socioeconomic predictor of healthy ageing. It has been shown that improving neighbourhood education can help individuals in the community, particularly those of lower education levels, to achieve person-environment fit, and this, together with improved neighbourhood socioeconomic status, is beneficial to healthy ageing (Lu et al., 2021).

While a consensus measure of healthy ageing has not been reached (Lu et al., 2021), growing old comes with multiple morbidities or chronic degenerative conditions and functional impairment because ageing is simply a natural process of wear and tear resulting in the degeneration of organs and systems of the human body. Intrinsic functions are related to relevant environmental and social characteristics surrounding individuals, whose socioeconomic and educational backgrounds prevail. Elderly health is a care business in maintaining bodily functioning with the aim to slow down the rate of deterioration, and, equally important, is the rehabilitation of impaired functions to allow for mobility, self-care, and independence in daily living. Ageing in place has been strongly promoted by academics and practitioners in aged care. Some governments have adopted this social need into the policy. It is important for older adults to spend the last stage of their lives in a familiar home and neighbourhood to make life easier and happier, and to avoid a need for adjustment to new places.

The authors advocate ageing with dignity because it is of utmost importance to live happily with dignity and respect in optimal health (Law & Fong, 2022). When one becomes dependent, one should receive humanistic care and services. Unfortunately, abusing older adults by carers, whether blood-related or on the payroll, is not uncommon in this civilised world, where many people and governments are talking about ethics and laws to protect their citizens, particularly the more vulnerable groups like the older adults, women, children, and ethnic minorities. To achieve healthy or successful ageing, an absence of disease, absence of disability, preserved cognitive performance, appropriate physical performance, and active social participation are the key and indispensable factors for individual older adults. Interventions must be engaged in moderation, which is one of Confucius' teaching about life.

While health and social care professionals provide care, older adults should take their personal responsibility in the pursuit of healthy ageing. For example, the doctor may prescribe medicines after consultation, but he or she has no control whatsoever over drug compliance, which it is a common patient behaviour. Similarly, if older adults do not follow professional instructions and if the family members or carers do not keep a close monitoring, then goodwill changes like lifestyle modifications will not happen. Standing community programmes in health education and awareness promotion with emphasis on personal responsibility and engagement are necessary to assure the success of healthy ageing. Self-management and self-care are promoted in aged care to enhance self-efficacy among older adults, who require training for the necessary skills to cope with and adapt to the "new" phase of life. They also need self-confidence and encouragement from the health and social care professionals, family members, carers, and neighbours.

Healthy ageing in the social perspective

Human societies are well structured and organised in social, political, and cultural contexts. Each society has its rules and regulations of operations in making decisions on social provisions according to the needs of the residents and the available resources. The law shapes the behaviour of the people and the overall orders of a community. Social relationships become an integral part of life. Community clanship has close lifelong influence on individuals because everyone lives and grows in a fairly well-defined community. Each resident has a role to play, either in leadership or ordinary citizenship. Everyone contributes to the society in different ways, even when they are old and have retired, for the benefits of individual's fulfilment, and collective tangible and intangible growths of the society. Older adults should be considered precious assets of the family and community. They can still contribute to the new role (World Health Organization, 2020). Truly, ageing should be a golden social opportunity.

Healthy ageing means different things in different societies and to different people. Moreover, the extent of socioeconomic inequalities in healthcare services may be different in different countries and regions due to the varied local situations in economic, political, cultural, and epidemiological origins and past histories (Lu et al., 2022). Older adults may feel good in making continuing contributions to the society they have been interacting with for their entire life. They may be assigned to new roles, being reshuffled into and out of positions within formal and informal organisations. Such changes in the society for older adults have implications, directly and indirectly, on community resource allocation. In some instances, retired people do not expect financial rewards from their continuing social participation, and hence they are complimentary to the social assets, which can be further enhanced by a social platform for cognitive training and stress sharing to support and manage interpersonal communications and social connectivity in an information-led society. These aims to sustain sociodemographic, psychological, physical, and behavioural factors are associated with better quality of life, and at the same time, supporting healthy ageing (Heshmati, 2016). All such social measures should not be overlooked or ignored by leaders of any society.

Many countries or regions are promoting healthy ageing and age-friendly communities. The society has the duty to promote the health and wellness of people according to the Sustainable Development Goal 3 proposed by the United Nations in 2015 (Fong et al., 2021). For instance, in Hong Kong, most of such programmes are delivered by NGOs with the support and monitoring of the Social Welfare Department of the Government. These organisations have been found to lack staff and expertise in the health-related side of healthy ageing although social care and attention to older adults and their families are excellent and comprehensive. Courses on the knowledge and management of common elderly conditions for social workers should be provided to enrich their understanding of the healthcare needs of older adults. More work needs to be done in nurturing medical-social collaboration in aged care to achieve healthy ageing.

Schools and workplaces are social institutions that can help nurture healthy ageing. Young people should be taught to respect the older generation. Through learning in service-learning subjects, young people change their perceptions about older people, who are not stubborn or apathetic. The intergenerational experience results in students' positive attitudes towards older adults in understanding their feelings and health issues. In the exercise, communication has been noted to be the key to building relationships. Students and older adults have built positive relationships and demonstrated effective communication skills such as active listening and showing empathy (Fong et al., 2023). Moreover, people spend a large part of their life, particularly waking hours, at the workplace, where a strategically and practically healthy work life should be promoted. Programmes, campaigns, and vocational training should target health maintenance. A healthy workplace is beneficial to the employers who save on medical benefits to the staff, and gain from enhanced productivity and reduced absenteeism and accidents. The atmosphere in the workplace becomes cheerful and is conducive to healthy ageing in later life after retirement of the employees. Employers should promote health in workplaces. They may consider working with insurance companies on such schemes.

In addition to the social trend, value, and local culture, the physical setting of age-friendly communities, barrier-free access facilities, like lifts, ramps, and dropped kerbs, are purposedly built to help older adults use the footbridges and subways to cross roads and gain access to buildings and facilities. Other installations, like lighting, colour contrast, resting places, soft and smooth surfaces, etc., provide a safe environment to avoid hazards and minimise accidents. All the community and social actions require leadership, good public education, community engagement, and support from local organisations, the private sector, academia, and professionals in health and social care. The main objectives are to enhance ageing in place and to promote healthy ageing. All these strategies require government and community support.

Healthy ageing in the economic perspective

Older adults may not contribute to the economy directly or in the usual sense of contributing to an economy. Ageing is often considered as counterproductive and is viewed negatively from the local economic perspective. While it is true that older adults are not active or productive in employment, they should not be regarded as a burden in the family or society or as a financial burden because they have retired from work. Conversely, an ageing population may contribute to the community in different ways.

It is a fact that older people suffer from chronic and degenerative conditions that require medical and social care as well as family attention. Such tasks involve social and financial input directly related to the healthcare and social welfare services, and indirectly to the opportunity cost of time cost to family members who take time off work or from home duties to care for the sick or frail older members of the family. Tang et al. have provided empirical evidence on the economic impact of population ageing. Their study states that the poor health of older adults in a population can be a critical factor in limiting economic growth. This is because the labour inputs in production are potentially crowded out by family caregiving (Tang et al., 2022). However, it has also been suggested that an ageing population does not necessarily cost a lot to care for (Normand et al., 2021; World Health Organization, n.d.). If older adults are kept fit, healthy, and active, then they can continue to be productive and contribute towards economic and societal benefits. It is a fact that the functional capability of an older adult is not directly related to their natural age. A recent study in Japan has shown that health interventions can generate economic benefits by reducing exits from the labour market due to health reasons, and by reducing expenditures in avoidable health services and long-term care (Okamoto et al., 2023).

The private sector has a role to play in healthy ageing from an economic perspective, particularly in the employment of older adults since business companies are more flexible in their human resources policy and arrangements. Continuing employment has a substantial effect on older adults in their health, social connectivity, living arrangements, and community participation. Healthy older adults can be engaged by these private companies to positions commensurate with their qualifications, experience, and capability in full-time or supplementary duties. Retired older adults are more interested in having something to do than in the financial reward. Many retired older adults serve as volunteers or employees of social enterprises, making a return to society by contributing their time and skills in work or services they can handle comfortably. Hence, it is good for the private sector to give older adults a chance and engage them appropriately. In this regard, the government should review the retirement policy and implement innovative alternatives for healthy older adults as part of a healthy ageing policy. A Chinese study has observed the benefits of investment in healthy and successful ageing, such as increased disposable incomes to pay for housing, transportation, health, and other social activities (Heshmati, 2016).

Healthy ageing in the political perspective

It is common for social activities to get involved in politics, which is intrinsic of human beings. Issues of healthy ageing are naturally linked to political consideration in the public view of the older population and policies concerning this group of seemingly unproductive members of the community. On top of being old and frail, older adults are commonly being marginalised by the society because of their age in the life course and lack of economic contribution. Abuse of older adults in the family and institutions is not new. It takes strong leadership to steer reasonable, positive, targeted, and appropriate policies for the promotion of healthy ageing.

There are inequalities among the older adults because of income, wealth, personal and family backgrounds, social support, etc. Governments provide subsidised accommodation, healthcare services, and financial assistance to those in need. For example, the Hong Kong Government has implemented the Public Transport Fare Concession Scheme for older adults in using public transport, the Elderly Health Care Voucher Scheme for older adults to consult health professionals in the private sector, subsidised residential homes, Social Security Allowance Scheme, and other assistance schemes targeted at older adults. Older adults in Hong Kong are also well looked after by the public healthcare services under the policy of 'no one will be deprived of appropriate treatment because of lack of means', even though they are not the influential stakeholders of the political system, which is executive-led, not voter-directed. It has been proposed that political issues in most policies are related to intragenerational inequity. Thus, the real causes of such and similar problems surrounding ageing must be well understood in making healthy and sustainable policies (Greer et al., 2022).

However, political identities, politics, and policies are not driven by ageing alone. For instance, it was noted that during the COVID-19 pandemic, the COVID virus was more dangerous to older people than the general population. Compounded by poor management of residential care homes, the morbidity of older adults was a major public concern, demonstrating the gross vulnerability of older adults in the community. A life-course approach in which welfare policies are designed to benefit both the old and the young generations. This will help narrow the intergenerational conflicts and distributional politics (Greer et al., 2022). In the Netherlands, intergenerational housing arrangements, known as Humanitas, are widely referred example of a long-term aged care model to manage the challenges of ageing in the community (Arentshorst et al., 2019).

Yoshino et al. (2019) recommend comprehensive structural reforms in the labour supply, welfare system, and macroeconomic policy for improving the quantity and quality of the labour force, public finance, and a comprehensive review of retirement schemes in measures like raising the retirement age and individual contributions. Well-managed schemes will contribute to national savings and investment, and lead to economic growth and financial sustainability. Thus, a healthy ageing policy is an efficient way to address the challenges of the increasing ageing population in the world. Appropriate strategies, resources, and practices will generate optimal long-term social and economic benefits in interpersonal communication, social connectedness, health-diet linkages, among the older adults (Heshmati, 2016).

With the increasing ageing population on Earth, aged care must always be a top priority policy consideration. Policies that are conducive to healthy ageing should take on a community-based, preventive, integrative, and positive approach. In addition, promotion of the positive aspects of ageing and encouragement of lifelong education, and community engagement in the social care of the older adults are equally important. In particular, education has been found to be the strongest predictor of healthy ageing (Lu et al., 2022). Financial support is a major concern among the older adults in life-long education (Law et al., 2023). Strategies, no matter how well-intended, are not good enough if they do not entail dignity and the humane perspective, which should be on the agenda of all stakeholders involved in the care and business of elderly services, such as the government, healthcare professionals, service providers, carers, and families.

Love, respect, and protect older adults

Governments need to enhance multisectoral collaboration in policy development and strengthen the health system building blocks, as well as formulate and implement the national work plan for an integrated community healthcare model designed for healthy ageing, which is safe, effective, person-centred, timely, equitable, and sustainable. The proposed goals should be specific, measurable, realistic, feasible, and time-bound. Regarding the future development of an integrated healthcare model for healthy ageing, the key characteristics of a community health model (Fong & Chiu, 2023), including availability, acceptability, accessibility, affordability, achievability, comprehensiveness, continuity, coordination, client-orientation, and cross-discipline, should be well considered.

It was a disturbing, distressing, and heart-breaking sight when older patients were left in the open areas outside the Accident and Emergency Departments of public hospitals in February 2022 in the early days of the fifth wave of the COVID-19 pandemic in Hong Kong. Although temporary make-shift shelters were provided, these sick older adults, mostly infected by the coronavirus, were waiting for hours and even a few days before they were admitted to the wards. The community got very angry. Many people wondered where the dignity of the older adults was when they were treated in such an inhumane manner. Traditional Chinese philosophy teaches us to treat the older adults as our own, no matter what. It is hoped that 'Love the elderly, respect the elderly, and protect the elderly' should be promoted as a dictum in caring for the older adults in the world.

References

Arentshorst, M. E., Kloet, R. R., & Peine, A. (2019). Intergenerational housing: The case of humanitas Netherlands. *Journal of Housing for the Elderly, 33*(3), 244–256. https://doi.org/10.1080/02763893.2018.1561592

Chung, R. Y. N., & Marmot, M. (2020). People in Hong Kong have the longest life expectancy in the world: Some possible explanations. *NAM Perspectives, 2020*. https://doi.org/10.31478%2F202001d

Fong, B. Y. F. (2022). Ageing and frailty. *Hong Kong Medical Journal, 28*(5), 344–346. https://doi.org/10.12809/hkmj215134

Fong, B. Y. F., & Chiu, W. K. (2023). A systems approach to achieving health for all in the community. In B. Y. F. Fong & W. C. W. Wong (Eds.), *Gaps and actions in health improvement from Hong Kong and beyond* (pp. 41–54). Springer. https://doi .org/10.1007/978-981-99-4491-0_4

Fong, B. Y. F., Law, V. T. S., Leung, T. C. H., Lo, M. F., Ng, T. K. C., & Yee, H. H. L. (2021). *Sustainable development goal 3 - Health and well-being of ageing in Hong Kong*. Routledge. https://doi.org/10.4324/9781003220169

Fong, B. Y. F., Yee, H. H. L., Ng, T. K. C., & Chiu, W. K. (2023). Intergenerational service-learning: An experience in Health Promotion among undergraduate students in Hong Kong. *Journal of Intergenerational Relationships*, 1–14. https://doi.org/10 .1080/15350770.2023.2172514

Greer, S. L., Lynch, J. F., Reeves, A., Raj, M., Gingrich, J., Falkenbach, M., ... Bambra, C. (2022). The politics of healthy ageing: Myths and realities. In *The politics of healthy ageing: Myths and realities*. European Observatory on Health Systems and Policies. https://www.ncbi.nlm.nih.gov/books/NBK583045

Heshmati, A. (2016). *The economics of healthy ageing in China*. IZA Discussion Paper No. 9713. https://dx.doi.org/10.2139/ssrn.2731976

Law, V. T. S., & Fong, B. Y. F. (Eds.). (2022). *Ageing with dignity in Hong Kong and Asia - Holistic and humanistic care*. Quality of Life in Asia Series. Springer.

Law, V. T. S., Yee, H. H. L., Ng, T. K. C., & Fong, B. Y. F. (2023). Evaluating the impact of lifelong education on older adults: A case study from Hong Kong. *Journal of Adult and Continuing Education*. https://doi.org/10.1177/14779714231156747

14   *Ben Y. F. Fong and Wang-Kin Chiu*

Leung, A. Y. M., Su, J. J., Lee, E. S. H., Fung, J. T. S., & Molassiotis, A. (2022). Intrinsic capacity of older people in the community using WHO Integrated Care for Older People (ICOPE) framework: A cross-sectional study. *BMC Geriatrics, 22*(1), Article 304. https://doi.org/10.1186/s12877-022-02980-1

Lu, C., Zong, J., Wang, L., Du, Y., & Wang, Q. (2022). Healthy aging index and its link with relative education between individual and neighborhood: A population-based, cohort study. *BMC Geriatrics, 22*(1), Article 778. https://doi.org/10.1186/s12877 -022-03469-7

Lu, W., Pikhart, H., & Sacker, A. (2021). Comparing socio-economic inequalities in healthy ageing in the United States of America, England, China and Japan: Evidence from four longitudinal studies of ageing. *Ageing & Society, 41*(7), 1495– 1520. https://doi.org/10.1017/S0144686X19001740

Normand, C., May, P., Johnston, B., & Cylus, J. (2021). *Health and social care near the end of life: Can policies reduce costs and improve outcomes?* European Observatory on Health Systems and Policies. https://iris.who.int/bitstream/handle/10665/349803 /Policy-brief-1997-8073-2021-1-eng.pdf?sequence=1

Okamoto, S., Sakamoto, H., Kamimura, K., Komamura, K., Kobayashi, E., & Liang, J. (2023). Economic effects of healthy ageing: Functional limitation, forgone wages, and medical and long-term care costs. *Health Economics Review, 13*(1), Article 28. https://doi.org/10.1186/s13561-023-00442-x

Tang, B., Li, Z., Hu, S., & Xiong, J. (2022). Economic implications of health care burden for elderly population. *Inquiry: The Journal of Health Care Organization, Provision, and Financing, 59.* https://doi.org/10.1177/00469580221121511

World Health Organization. (2020). *Healthy ageing and functional ability.* https://www .who.int/news-room/questions-and-answers/item/healthy-ageing-and-functional -ability

World Health Organization. (n.d.). *Economics of healthy and active ageing.* https://eur ohealthobservatory.who.int/themes/observatory-programmes/health-and-economy/ economics-of-ageing

Yoshino, N., Kim, C. J., & Sirivunnabood, P. (2019). The aging population and its impacts on fiscal sustainability. In *Aging societies - Policies and perspectives.* Asian Development Bank Institute. https://www.adb.org/sites/default/files/publication /543006/adbi-aging-societies-policies-and-perspectives.pdf

2 Policy analysis of COVID-19 pandemic in Hong Kong, China, based on the multiple streams framework

Vincent T. S. Law and Ben Y. F. Fong

Abstract

In February 2020, the World Health Organization (WHO) named the new virus Coronavirus Disease 2019 (COVID-19) and declared the outbreak a world pandemic in March 2020. After three and a half years, the COVID-19 remains an acute global emergency. As of 1 November 2023, the global number of confirmed cases had reached 771.55 million while the death toll had reached 6.97 million, and 13,533,465,652 vaccine doses had been administered. The WHO published eight policy briefs for global policymakers to adopt locally to fight against COVID-19. However, older adults all over the world have suffered seriously from the COVID-19 and their death toll is far higher than that of any other age bands. In Hong Kong, the government once implemented one of the strictest anti-pandemic measures in the world, including border closure, social distancing, compulsory quarantine and isolation, compulsory testing, and voluntary COVID-19 vaccination. Nevertheless, Hong Kong has been seriously affected by five infection waves of the COVID-19, especially during the fifth wave of COVID-19 which started on 31 December 2021. As of 1 November 2023, the number of confirmed cases had reached 2,880,021 while the death toll had reached 13,825. In the fifth wave of COVID-19 infection, the number of confirmed cases and death toll in Hong Kong had reached 1,549,445 and 11,991 which constituted 56.5% and 98.3% of the total respectively. Among the death cases in the fifth wave, 87% of the deaths were aged 70 years or above. During the COVID-19 pandemic, healthy ageing could not be guaranteed due to the breakdown of health systems and stringent social isolation of older adults. Since 2022, increasingly more societies have adopted a living with COVID-19 policy to resume normal economic and social activities. Following Mainland China's dynamic zero-COVID policy closely, Hong Kong has been very prudent in fighting against the COVID-19 pandemic and somewhat sluggish in relaxing anti-pandemic measures in the later half of 2022. In January 2023, Hong Kong followed Mainland China and greatly relaxed its anti-pandemic measures against COVID-19. Based on John Kingdon's Multiple Streams Framework (MSF), this chapter analyses the influence of COVID-19 infection on Hong Kong and the anti-pandemic

DOI: 10.4324/9781003436881-2

policy measures that have been implemented. The chapter ends by recommending post-pandemic policies to promote healthy ageing and proactive preparation for future epidemics or pandemics for the benefit of Hong Kong.

COVID-19 pandemic in Hong Kong

Brief summary of government measures

The preparation against COVID-19 infection in Hong Kong started in December 2019 when a cluster of pneumonia cases was reported in Wuhan city of Mainland China (HKSAR Government, 2019). Three and a half years later, the Government of the Hong Kong Special Administrative Region (HKSAR) lowered the response level under the Preparedness and Response Plan for Novel Infectious Disease of Public Health Significance from the Emergency to Alert level in May 2023. The latter marked the significant step of Hong Kong to resume normalcy in various aspects after the COVID-19 pandemic. A brief timeline (December 2019 to May 2023) with major events and government measures in Hong Kong during the COVID-19 pandemic is summarised in **Table 2.1.**

Influence of COVID-19 infection on Hong Kong

The outbreak of COVID-19 was first reported in December 2019. On 11 March 2020, the World Health Organization (WHO) declared the outbreak of the COVID-19 as a pandemic (WHO, 2023a). The new coronavirus is highly contagious and causes respiratory infections with symptoms ranging from common cold to more severe symptoms like the severe acute respiratory syndrome (SARS) (WHO, 2023b). As of 1 November 2023, there were 771,549,718 confirmed cases of COVID-19, including 6,974,473 deaths reported to the WHO, and 13,533,465,652 vaccine doses administered (WHO, 2023b). Although the global cumulative death rate is only 0.90%, the COVID-19 has caused unprecedented disturbance to economy, society, and public policy globally over the three years.

The SARS-CoV-2 virus is mainly transmitted via air or contact with respiratory droplets. Many infected people experience no symptoms or mild symptoms in the early stage while the estimated incubation period ranges from 1 to 14 days (HKSAR Government, 2023a). However, the death rate among the infected older adults with chronic diseases is very high. To fight against the COVID-19, different countries or regions have adopted various measures which include lockdown, quarantine, social distancing, curfew, wearing of masks, and vaccination.

Number of COVID-19 infections (January 2020–September 2023)

According to the statistics of notifiable infectious diseases of the Centre for Health Protection of Hong Kong, there was a total of 2,880,021 infected cases

Table 2.1 A Brief Summary of Government Measures during COVID-19 Pandemic in Hong Kong (December 2019 to May 2023)

Time	Events or Government Measures
31 December 2019	The HKSAR Government announced the close monitoring of a cluster of pneumonia cases in a local seafood market reported in Wuhan city of Mainland China (HKSAR Government, 2019).
22 January 2020	The HKSAR Government announced the first suspected case of COVID-19 of a 39-year-old male who had travelled from Wuhan to Shenzhen, and then to Hong Kong via High Speed Rail on 21 January 2020 (HKSAR Government, 2020a).
4 February 2020	The HKSAR Government announced its investigatiof on three additional COVID-positive cases which were later confirmed to be local confirmed cases. This marked the first local spread of COVID-19 in Hong Kong (HKSAR Government, 2020b).
20 December 2021	A South Asian woman was infected by two other South Asian residents of a quarantine hotel at Yau Ma Tei. She infected five family members. Then her husband infected over hundreds of residents of Kwai Chung Estate (Cheung et al., 2022). This marked the start of the 5th wave of COVID-19 pandemic and heavy death tolls in Hong Kong.
	During the 5th wave (since 31 December 2021) of pandemic in Hong Kong, there were 81,117 imported cases and 3,012,831 locally acquired cases, totalling 3,093,948 cases tested positive for SARS-CoV-2 virus by nucleic acid tests and rapid antigen tests (CHP, 2023a).
16 January 2023	The HKSAR Government announced that the evaluation criteria for COVID-19 nucleic acid test results would be adjusted (HKSAR Government, 2023e). Test results issued with a Ct value of 35 or above would be regarded as COVID-negative for purposes other than clinical management.
19 January 2023	The HKSAR Government announced the cancellation of arrangements for issuing isolation orders to COVID-infected persons according to the Prevention and Control of Disease Regulation (Cap. 599A) from 30 January 2023 since Omicron became the predominant variant of the COVID-19 virus, enhanced prevention and treatment capacities of the healthcare system, and reduced the risk posted by COVID-19 to the local public health (HKSAR Government, 2023f). This was a significant step towards resumption of normalcy.
28 February 2023	The HKSAR Government announced that all mandatory mask-wearing requirements will be lifted with effect from 1 March 2023, thus Hong Kong has started to resume full normalcy after three years of COVID-19 pandemic (HKSAR Government, 2023g).
5 May 2023	The WHO announced that COVID-19 had become an established and ongoing health issue. It no longer constituted a public health emergency of international concern (PHEIC) (WHO, 2023c).
30 May 2023	The HKSAR Government lowered the response level under the Preparedness and Response Plan for Novel Infectious Disease of Public Health Significance from the Emergency to Alert level, being a major milestone in Hong Kong's anti-pandemic measures over three years (HKSAR Government, 2023h). Hong Kong resumes normalcy in various aspects.

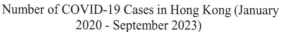

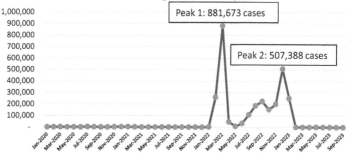

Figure 2.1 Number of COVID-19 Infected Cases in Hong Kong (January 2020– September 2023)

of COVID-19 during January 2020 and September 2023 (CHP, 2023b). As shown in **Figure 2.1**, the two peaks of COVID-19 infection in Hong Kong were March 2022 (with 881,673 infected cases) and December 2022 (with 507,388 infected cases).

(Source: CHP, 2023b)

Implementation of anti-pandemic measures

In Hong Kong, the HKSAR government adopted measures such as border closure, wearing of masks, social distancing, compulsory testing of designated groups, compulsory isolation, and voluntary vaccination. The effectiveness and policy implications of such anti-pandemic measures are analysed through John W. Kingdon's multiple streams framework (MSF).

John Kingdon's multiple streams framework

According to John W. Kingdon (Kingdon, 2011; Sapru, 2017), the public policymaking process can be viewed as a product of interaction between three distinct and partially independent streams, namely the problem stream, policy stream, and political stream, which can be analysed based on a multiple streams framework (MSF). Each stream can be analysed through some distinct but dynamic factors. For the problem stream, indicators, focussing events, crises, feedback, and problem definition are evidence to focus on (Kingdon, 2011). Regarding the policy stream, factors to consider include technical feasibility, value congruence, public acceptance, and knowledge about the policy issue. The political stream, the third stream, focusses on public mood, interest groups, and consensus building.

The MSF has been used extensively in the analysis of various public policy issues, for example, the role of experts in environmental change (Valin & Huitema, 2023), policy changes towards sustainability (Derwort et al., 2022), policy decision process of the European Union (Ackrill et al., 2013), as well as policy on carbon dioxide emissions of the United Kingdom (Cooper-Searle et al., 2018). For health-related policies, the MSF has also been applied to analyse the role of institutional entrepreneurs in primary healthcare (Smith & Cumming, 2017), problems and policy responses of setting up drug consumption rooms in Finland (Unlu et al., 2022), setting of the policy agenda for hepatitis C virus in Switzerland (Kind et al., 2022), policy opportunities to adopt telehealth (Giese, 2020), as well as setting of the policy agenda of an electronic referral system in Iran (Kabir et al., 2022). Since the MSF overcomes the problems of other theories for policy analysis and provides different solutions for any policy issues (Hoefer, 2022), the MSF was used to analyse the policymaking process of anti-pandemic policy measures against COVID-19 in Hong Kong during late 2019 and 2023.

Policy analysis of COVID-19 measures in Hong Kong

Problem stream

For the problem stream, people must recognise there is a policy problem to solve (Kingdon, 2011; Sapru, 2017). During the COVID-19 pandemic in Hong Kong, policymakers have had to fix the problems caused by the extensive spreading of the SARS-CoV-2 virus, intensifying fear of infection, quarantine, and health complications, rising death tolls (especially among the older adults), as well as negative economic and social lives.

Indicator changes

On 22 January 2020, the HKSAR government announced the first suspected case of COVID-19 of a Hong Kong citizen who had travelled to Wuhan and Shenzhen before returning to Hong Kong. This indicated the formal start of the breakout of COVID-19 in Hong Kong.

Initially, the panic among Hong Kong citizens was mild. However, the number of cases continued to rise. Between 23 January 2020 and 29 January 2023, there were a total of 1,226,467 and 1,880,112 cases tested positive by nucleic acid tests and rapid antigen tests (RATs), respectively, for the SARS-CoV-2 virus, contributing to a total of 3,106,579 cases (CHP, 2023a).

Hong Kong learnt a painful lesson during the fifth wave (since 31 December 2021) of the COVID-19 pandemic in Hong Kong. During 31 December 2021 and 29 January 2023, there were a total of 1,203,020 and

1,660,455 cases tested positive by nucleic acid tests and rapid antigen tests (RATs), respectivel,y for the SARS-CoV-2 virus, contributing to a total of 2,863,475 cases (CHP, 2023a). However, a total of 13,120 death cases was recorded during this period. Among the death toll during this period, the number of deaths of the 60–69, 70–79, and 80 years or above age bands were 1,150 (8.8% of the total), 2,159 (16.5% of the total), and 9,246 (70.5% of the total), respectively. The percentage of death cases for infected persons aged 60 years or above constituted 95.7% of the total. The vast increase in the total number of infected cases and death rates among the older persons indicated the apex of COVID-19 infection among Hong Kong citizens during the fifth wave and doubt about the effectiveness of anti-pandemic measures.

Problem definition

Since December 2019, the HKSAR government has been re-defining the problems related to the COVID-19 pandemic. In early January 2020, the policy problem was to try every means to stop imported cases. As the number of infections arose over time, the measure changed to contain the import of infected cases by stringent border control and compulsory quarantine of the infected persons by prompt identification and treatment. After the fifth wave of infection was stabilised in May 2022, while observing a small peak of infection during November 2022 and January 2023, the problem then switched to formulating measures to resume normalcy in economic and social perspectives.

Focussing event (crisis)

Hong Kong encountered a massive COVID-19 wave due to the Omicron variants in January 2022 (Ioannidis et al., 2023) which marked the start of the fifth wave of infection. Public hospitals were crowded with infected patients and they could not handle the large influx. Patients, especially older adults, were forced to wait outdoors for hours or even overnight for accident and emergency services of public hospitals during cold weather. In the extreme cases, the public hospitals could not handle the rising death tolls while dead bodies lay on the floor of hospital wards near the hospitalised patients. The pandemic crisis reached its apex during the fifth wave of COVID-19 pandemic and became one of the focussing events or crises in the public health history of Hong Kong.

Among various crises, Hong Kong citizens also faced a social crisis of 'anti-pandemic fatigue' and a mental crisis. During the peak waves of COVID-19 pandemic, Hong Kong faced virtually complete lockdown, which cast negative economic and social consequences (Chan et al., 2021). Due to COVID-19 restrictions, citizens were both mentally and physically exhausted (Haktanir et al., 2022; Tee et al., 2020; Vindegaard et al., 2020), psychologically distressed, and were lonely (McGinty et al., 2020). Under strict anti-pandemic measures, Hong Kong citizens once saw no hope for the resumption of normal activities and felt desperate even though they followed the anti-pandemic measures strictly (Vindegaard et al., 2020).

Healthcare professionals also experienced high levels of burnout during the COVID-19 pandemic since they had to work long hours, work in a high-risk environment, have inadequate and insufficient resources, as well as increased workloads (Galanis et al., 2021). Besides, the employed or those who were self-employed found it challenging to recover from mental stress if they stayed self-employed longer (Lee et al., 2020).

Politically and socially, citizens' trust in the government, the media, and limited health concerns were also affected by their own subjective well-being (Anastasiou & Duquenne, 2021). This was reflected in the initial fear about compulsory quarantine in community quarantine facilities and voluntary vaccination, which were measures to protect lives.

Feedback

As advocated by Chan et al. (2021), the interaction between government and public responses has stimulated the reassessment of mitigation strategies that can strengthen the capability and further improve the effectiveness of response measures in controlling future epidemics or pandemics (Verlinghieri, 2020). During the COVID-19 pandemic in Hong Kong, government departments or units, in particular the Centre for Health Protection (CHP), played a vital role in disseminating the latest COVID-19 infection situations and anti-pandemic measures in Hong Kong.

Right before the first case of COVID-19 infection was reported in Hong Kong on 22 January 2020, the CHP published the 'Guidelines on the Prevention of Coronavirus Disease 2019 (COVID-19) for the General Public' to provide knowledge to the general public about the virus (CHP, 2023a). An up-to-date website and an integrated dashboard for COVID-19, which included information of each confirmed case, for example, onset and confirmation date of infection, gender, age, location, etc., was launched for timely access by the general public.

The government received feedback from the media and the general public via multiple channels. Such feedback partly helped the formulation of timely and effective policy measures for the government but might be more important in serving as channels for the general public to release pressure exerted by the stringent anti-pandemic measures.

Policy stream

For the policy stream, formal policies emerge from an array of policy ideas proposed by the policy community (Kingdon, 2011; Sapru, 2017). Both government intervention and community engagement are vital in the effective implementation of any public health intervention (WHO, 2020a). Among the major stakeholders of the policy community in Hong Kong, government officials and health experts played the most important roles as policy entrepreneurs in advocating policy solutions to tackle the various problems caused by the COVID-19 pandemic. They invested resources to advocate and lobby support for policy measures and contributed to formulating and implementing policy measures related to the combat against COVID-19 and the subsequent resumption of normalcy for Hong Kong.

Technical feasibility of COVID-19 measures

It is imperative to adjust public health strategies in view of the changing public attitudes towards public health measures (Voo et al., 2021). In Hong Kong, one of the major controversies in policy measures during the COVID-19 pandemic was the choice between 'living with COVID' policy and 'zero-COVID' policy.

As a Special Administrative Region of China, Hong Kong adopted far less strict measures to contain COVID-19 than the counterpart provinces and cities in Mainland China (Chan et al., 2021) in the early onset of the COVID-19 pandemic. In particular, the Hong Kong government and citizens held the collective memories of combating the outbreak of severe acute respiratory syndrome (SARS) in 2003 (Chan et al., 2021). During the onset of COVID-19 pandemic, the government adopted preventive education, publicity, and various control measures which were regarded as vital contributors to the success of controlling SARS in 2003 (Hung, 2003). The strict containing policy for the COVID-19 started in January 2020 when the Hong Kong Government adopted measures to partially lock down the city (Ho & Chan, 2021). However, Hong Kong's public transportation systems and public facilities are superspreading environments (Loo et al., 2021), in conjunction with Hong Kong's crowded living and working environments, contributed to the extensive spreading of the COVID-19 virus during the fourth and fifth waves of the pandemic. In April 2022, Hong Kong followed the zero-COVID policy and adopted the test-trace-isolate-quarantine (TTIQ) strategy that cases tested positive with COVID-19 were isolated from the main community, their close contacts were traced and identified for compulsory quarantine. Besides, flights from high-risk nations were suspended (Lau et al., 2022).

China stuck to the zero-COVID-19 policy for almost three years during the COVID-19 pandemic where strict lockdowns, many at the community levels, and other aggressive restrictive measures were taken (Ioannidis et al., 2023). In April 2022, the Chinese Government decided to pursue the national dynamic zero-COVID-19 policy which used massive testing and strict quarantine measures to minimise any outbreak of COVID-19 virus before its spreading (Burki, 2022). On 7 December 2022, China's National Health Commission announced key changes to the national policy on COVID-19. Individuals who were asymptomatic or had mild symptoms of COVID-19 were permitted to isolate at home rather than in designated quarantine facilities. Lockdowns were only targeted at high-risk zones or specific buildings and would be discontinued after five days without any new cases of COVID-19 (Burki, 2023). With this major move away from the zero-COVID-19 policy in China, Hong Kong also relaxed its restrictive policy in early 2023.

Wearing of masks

At the onset of the COVID-19 spread, wearing masks was not mandatory and even not a universal recommendation by the WHO. There were concerns that mask wearing could engender a false sense of security in relation to other methods of infection control (for example, social distancing and handwashing) (Cheng et al., 2022). In April 2020, the WHO's interim guidance did not yet recommend the massive use of face masks for healthy individuals in the community as a way to prevent infection with COVID-19 (WHO, 2020b). It was also found that controlling harm at source by mask wearing is at least as important as mitigation, for example handwashing (Cheng et al., 2022). The use of surgical masks due to an increasing awareness of personal hygiene had emerged as common practices for citizens in Hong Kong (Ho & Chan, 2021). Mass masking for source control is a useful and low-cost adjunct to social distancing and hand hygiene during the COVID-19 pandemic (Cheng et al., 2022). In early 2020, Hong Kong citizens panicked to buy anti-pandemic commodities which included masks, alcohol sanitisers, and painkillers. Starting from 1 March 2023, the government has lifted the mask-wearing requirement after assessing the overall COVID-19 situation in Hong Kong (HKSAR Government, 2023g). This marked the migration to resumption of normalcy for Hong Kong citizens in their daily lives.

Social distancing and banning of public gatherings

Hong Kong once implemented one of the strictest social-distancing measures in the world. In 2020, according to the Prevention and Control of Disease (Prohibition on Group Gathering) Regulation (Cap. 599G), public gatherings of more than four people were prohibited. Offenders could face a maximum fine of $25,000 and/or imprisonment for up to six months. The widespread implementation of physical distancing during the COVID-19 pandemic, for example, work from home (WFH), distance learning, online shopping, food delivery, etc., had reshaped the mobility pattern of Hong Kong and became its new normal in the post-pandemic era (Chan et al., 2021).

Public acceptance of contact-tracing app

Among the anti-pandemic measures of Hong Kong, the implementation of a contact-tracing app, i.e., the 'LeaveHomeSafe', was controversial and aroused discussion on violation of personal privacy. The 'LeaveHomeSafe' mobile app was developed by the Hong Kong government for scanning and storing information of entry into premises. Although the use of the app was not compulsory, it was highly encouraged.

Although contact-tracing is an efficient and necessary strategy to disrupt the transmission chain of COVID-19, it demands enormous resources to be effective (Zhang et al., 2021). Besides, the sociopolitical context in public perception of public health measures is important (Voo et al., 2021). According to the survey by Voo et al. (2021), approximately 60% of the Hong Kong respondents regarded the use of digital contact-tracing as most disagreed among four measures. Hong Kong citizens showed more resistance against digital contact-tracing app than their counterparts in other Asian economies such as Malaysia, Singapore, and South Korea (Huang et al., 2021).

Voluntary COVID-19 vaccination

Initially with a low COVID-19 vaccination rate, Hong Kong has been very successful in encouraging voluntary vaccination during the COVID-19 pandemic by both legal and educational measures. According to Cap. 599K Prevention and Control of Disease (Use of Vaccines) Regulation (HKSAR Government, 2023b) of Hong Kong, the Secretary for Health may, on application, authorise a non-registered vaccine for a specific purpose for preventing, protecting against, delaying, or otherwise controlling the incidence or transmission of the specified disease. It has been advocated that COVID-19 vaccination can protect oneself and others. Vaccination can reduce length of stay in breakthrough infections and thus it helps prevent severe infections (Chen et al., 2023). Enhanced vaccination in older adults may improve turnover in hospital beds, which in particular helps relieve pressure on hospitals during the peak of the pandemic when there are a large number of more severe infections (Chen et al., 2023).

To safeguard public health and to allow the resuming of normal activities, the HKSAR government implemented a territory-wide COVID-19 Vaccination Programme free of charge for all Hong Kong residents since February 2021 (HKSAR Government, 2023c). As of 29 October 2023, the total doses of COVID-19 vaccines administered were 20,872,991. Among the citizens who got vaccinated, the population with first dose, second dose, and third dose were 6,917,853, 6,801,763, and 5,858,894, respectively, representing 94.6%, 93.0%, and 80.1% of the population aged 6 months or above. Among them, 1,690,247 (77.0% of the citizens aged 60 years or above) had gotten vaccinated with the third dose of vaccine

(HKSAR Government, 2023d). This greatly reduced the hazard of health complications and death tolls.

Value congruence

East Asian cultures are traditionally heavily influenced by Confucianist beliefs which strongly emphasise social responsibility and collective good. Hence, citizens of East Asia, including Hong Kong, generally accept more intrusive and strict public health care policies being imposed by the government during the pandemic (Wang, 2020). A socio-culturally accepted practice such as personal and public hygiene in East Asia, for example, wearing of face masks, helped reduce the spread of COVID-19 virus (Wang, 2020). As compared with most of their Western counterparts, the East Asian cultures demonstrated a more coordinated and effective public health policy involving quarantine, district- or city-lockdown, and social distancing (Wang, 2020). The general public also trusted the majority of the medical experts of Hong Kong and thus enabled quick and direct application of evolving medical expertise into public health policies (Wang, 2020). This value congruence in Hong Kong contributed to the success of anti-pandemic measures in Hong Kong.

Political stream

The political stream sets the government agenda for the COVID-19 measures (Kingdon, 2011; Sapru, 2017). During the COVID-19 pandemic in Hong Kong, views of the health experts and consensus building were among the important elements that contributed to the success of resumption of normal.

Health experts as an influential interest group

When seeking solutions, governments can delegate power to experts, thus reducing or annulling social conflicts (Flinders & Dimova, 2020). Positive health experts' communication helps increase the support for banning public assembly (Yuen et al., 2023). Sometimes it is doubtful whether health experts can be involved for garnering support for unpopular health measures without risking public trust in them (Yuen et al., 2023). Even among public policymakers and health experts, reaching consensus is difficult due to diverging views (Antoci et al., 2022). Sometimes, opinions among health experts may also diverge, and the general public finds it difficult to follow (Lavazza & Farina, 2020). This was the case in Hong Kong while various health experts gave their personal views on the media daily but there was never a consensus.

However, the cases of the UK and the US showed that a COVID-19 policy supported by a health expert received greater public support as compared to a policy supported only by lawmakers (Arceneaux et al., 2020). Policymakers have to consider diverse interests of society, including economic, political, social, and administrative aspects, while health experts tend to give issue-specific recommendations based on individual expertise (Moore & MacKenzie, 2020). One of the effective anti-pandemic measures is to delegate strategies and decision-making of public policies to health experts who serve as government advisors or members of strategic committees. This was the case in Hong Kong during the pandemic and was proven to be effective. During the COVID-19 pandemic in Hong Kong, health experts such as Professor David Shu-cheong Hui of The Chinese University of Hong Kong, Professor Yuen Kwok-yung, Professor Lau Yu-lung, and Professor Hung Fan Ngai Ivan of The University of Hong Kong, have been prominent and served as advisors to the government. In Hong Kong, the general public generally believed in the advice of the health experts and adaptively complied with their advice during the COVID-19 pandemic.

Policy windows and policy entrepreneurs

On 1 July 2022, John Lee Ka-chiu, the former Secretary for Security, served as the Chief Executive of the HKSAR while Professor Lo Chung-mau, a world-renowned expert in liver transplant, served as the Secretary for Health. Between December 2019 and June 2022, the counterparts of John Lee and Professor Lo, that is, Carrie Lam Cheng Yuet-ngor (the former Chief Executive) and Professor Sophia Chan Siu-chee (the former Secretary of Food and Health) struggled against the COVID-19 pandemic during nearly two-thirds of their five-year term of office. Only six months after John Lee's administration was in place, the HKSAR government cancelled the arrangement of issuing isolation orders to COVID-infected persons on 19 January 2023 (HKSAR Government, 2023f). This remarkably mitigated the fear of Hong Kong citizens being compulsorily isolated in community quarantine facilities. Subsequently, the government lifted all mandatory mask-wearing requirements with effect from 1 March 2023 (HKSAR Government, 2023g) and lowered the response level under the Preparedness and Response Plan for Novel Infectious Disease of Public Health Significance from the Emergency to Alert level on 30 May 2023 (HKSAR Government, 2023h).

Riding on the decline of infected cases and lowered death toll after the first peak of the fifth wave of the pandemic in May 2022, the series of government measures under the new term of government were effective in combating the COVID-19 pandemic. The new government successfully utilised the changing epidemiological situations, social perception about COVID-19 infection, as well as, most importantly, the convergence of the three streams (that is, problem stream, policy stream, and political stream) (Kingdon, 2011; Sapru, 2017). John Lee and Professor Lo acted as the policy entrepreneurs who utilised the policy window to contain COVID-19 and paved the way to resumption of normal in 2023.

Recommendations

Policy on healthy ageing

The COVID-19 pandemic in Hong Kong demonstrated the persistence of serious social inequalities during major crises, and it is imperative to formulate policies to tackle inequalities (Béland et al., 2021). Health inequalities become even more apparent during the COVID-19 pandemic with individuals from ethnic minority groups, poorer socioeconomic statuses, and vulnerable groups of society (Mishra et al., 2021). Among the disadvantaged groups, the older adults have suffered from much higher death rates than other age bands during COVID-19, in particular those living in nursing homes (Béland & Marier, 2020). It is imperative to provide extra support to promote the well-being of citizens, especially those in disadvantaged situations during and after the COVID-19 pandemic (Yu & Du, 2022). Based on the analysis of John Kingdon's MSF, the older adults in Hong Kong are the key sufferers in terms of infection and death.

Various policy stakeholders such as government authorities, officials, healthcare professionals, and researchers should continue to play a vital role in formulating more proactive and visionary policies to promote public health and, in particular policy on healthy ageing. The Hong Kong government and the proximal policy stakeholders should conduct a comprehensive policy review on residential care for the older adults. In particular, infection control and outbreak management are among the target areas to be reviewed and improved. Ultimately, the service providers and students of healthcare-related programmes should be provided with training and drills on crisis and disaster management. Besides, public education on communicable diseases and community engagement in primary healthcare should also be greatly strengthened.

Policy on preparedness for future pandemics

The COVID-19 pandemic attracts increasing attention from various policy stakeholders (including government officials, academics, and the general public) to the relationship between social responses and policies (Chan et al., 2021). As advocated by Capano et al. (2022), policymakers are faced with increased uncertainty due to large-scale crises and thus need to explore new policy solutions (Capano et al., 2022). During the pandemic, various policy stakeholders such as government authorities, officials, healthcare professionals, researchers, and the general public collectively played important roles in effective risk communication and preparedness planning (Ratneswaren, 2020).

The COVID-19 pandemic prompts governments to conduct a critical review of urban transportation and its role in society among external hazards (Chan et al., 2021). Despite advocacy by pressure groups and health experts who are government's close aides during the COVID-19 pandemic, the government declined comprehensive review of the effectiveness and efficiency of its policy measures during the COVID-19 pandemic.

The Hong Kong government may take reference of Kidd's (2000) suggestions on preparing for future epidemics or pandemics by considering the principles of the Australian government such as: (1) protection of vulnerable people; (2) provision of treatment and support services to affected people; (3) continuity of regular healthcare services for the whole population; (4) protection and support of primary healthcare workers and primary care services; and (5) provision of mental health services to the community and the primary healthcare workforce.

With a long-term orientation, the ancient Chinese people promoted the concept of 'repairs the house before it rains' (see the Owl chapter of the classic Chinese literature Book of Songs). Learnt from the painful experience of the COVID-19 pandemic between 2019 and 2023, policymakers should be open-minded to proactively plan for future epidemics or pandemics—preparation for the future is never wrong and should never be too late.

Conclusion

The outbreak of the new virus Coronavirus Disease 2019 (COVID-19) has cast an unprecedented public health crisis on the world. The older adults all over the world have suffered seriously from the COVID-19 pandemic and their death toll is far higher than any other age bands. Hong Kong is no exception and has learnt a painful lesson from the pandemic since December 2019. In Hong Kong, the government once implemented one of the strictest measures in the world, including border closure, social distancing, long quarantine and isolation, compulsory testing, and voluntary vaccination. Nevertheless, Hong Kong was still seriously affected by the COVID-19, especially during the fifth wave of COVID-19 since 31 December 2021.

Based on John Kingdon's multiple streams framework (MSF), this chapter analyses the influence of COVID-19 infection on Hong Kong and the anti-pandemic measures that have been implemented. It was found that the health experts in Hong Kong, as one of the influential groups, played a very important role in combating the COVID-19 pandemic. Hong Kong citizens, being strongly influenced by East Asian culture of social responsibility and collective good, also partly contributed to the success of the anti-pandemic measures. Although certain policy measures such as contact-tracing app and compulsory quarantine and isolation once generated fear and doubt among Hong Kong citizens, the senior government officials of the HKSAR government utilised the convergence of the three streams (i.e., problem stream, policy stream, and political stream), a policy window, to gradually bring Hong Kong back to normal.

The concept of a global healthcare community should be integrated into public health policy. Hong Kong should serve as a benevolent and responsible neighbour to our geographical neighbours in the public health realms. In this regard, policymakers, health experts, and academics, in consultation with the general public, should formulate policy on healthy ageing for the older adults of Hong Kong, as well as being open-minded to get prepared for future epidemics or pandemics. Learnt from the painful experience of the COVID-19 pandemic between 2019 and 2023, policymakers should be open-minded to proactively plan for future epidemics or pandemics—preparation for the future is never wrong and should never be too late.

References

Ackrill, R., Kay, A., & Zahariadis, N. (2013). Ambiguity, multiple streams, and EU policy. *Journal of European Public Policy, 20*(6), 871–887. https://doi.org/10.1080/13501763.2013.781824

Anastasiou, E., & Duquenne, M.-N. (2021). First-Wave COVID-19 pandemic in Greece: The role of demographic, social, and geographical factors in life satisfaction during lockdown. *Social Sciences, 10*(6), 186. https://doi.org/10.3390/socsci10060186

Antoci, A., Sabatini, F., Sacco, P. L., & Sodini, M. (2022). Experts vs. policymakers in the COVID-19 response. *Journal of Economic Behavior & Organization, 201,* 22–39. https://doi.org/10.1016/j.jebo.2022.06.031

Arceneaux, K., Bakker, B. N., Hobolt, S., & De Vries, C. E. (2020). *Is COVID-19 a threat to liberal democracy.*

Béland, D., Cantillon, B., Hick, R., & Moreira, A. (2021). Social policy in the face of a global pandemic: Policy responses to the COVID-19 crisis. *Social Policy & Administration, 55*(2), 249–260. https://doi.org/10.1111/spol.12718

Béland, D., & Marier, P. (2020). COVID-19 and long-term care policy for older people in Canada. *Journal of Aging & Social Policy, 32*(4–5), 358–364. https://doi.org/10.1080/08959420.2020.1764319

Burki, T. (2022). Dynamic zero COVID policy in the fight against COVID. *Lancet. Respiratory Medicine, 10*(6), e58–e59. https://doi.org/10.1016/S2213-2600(22)00142-4

Burki, T. (2023). Moving away from zero COVID in China. *The Lancet: Respiratory Medicine, 11*(2), 132. https://doi.org/10.1016/S2213-2600(22)00508-2

Capano, G., Howlett, M., Jarvis, D. S. L., & Ramesh, M. (2022). Long-term policy impacts of the coronavirus: Normalization, adaptation, and acceleration in the post-COVID state. *Policy and Society, 41*(1), 1–12. https://doi.org/10.1093/polsoc/puab018

Centre for Health Protection (CHP), & Department of Health, Hong Kong Special Administrative Region. (2023a). *Situation of COVID-19 (23 January 2020 to 29 January 2023).* https://www.chp.gov.hk/en/features/102997.html

Centre for Health Protection (CHP), & Department of Health, Hong Kong Special Administrative Region. (2023b). *Number of notifiable infectious diseases by month.* https://www.chp.gov.hk/en/static/24012.html

Chan, H. Y., Chen, A., Ma, W., Sze, N. N., & Liu, X. T. (2021). COVID-19, community response, public policy, and travel patterns: A tale of Hong Kong. *Transport Policy, 106*, 173–184. https://doi.org/10.1016/j.tranpol.2021.04.002

Chen, D. X., Cowling, B., J., Ainslie, K. E. C., Yun, L., Wong, J. Y., Lau, E. H. Y., Wu, P., & Nealon, J. (2023). *Association of COVID-19 vaccination with duration of hospitalization in older adults in Hong Kong: A retrospective cohort study.* http://doi.org/10.2139/ssrn.4438013

Cheng, K. K., Lam, T. H., Leung, C., & C. (2022). Wearing face masks in the community during the COVID-19 pandemic: Altruism and solidarity. *The Lancet, 399*(10336), e39–e40. https://doi.org/10.1016/S0140-6736(20)30918-1

Cheung, H. P. H., Chan, C. P., & Jin, D. Y. (2022). Lessons learned from the fifth wave of COVID-19 in Hong Kong in early 2022. *Emerging Microbes & Infections, 11*(1), 1072–1078. https://doi.org/10.1080/22221751.2022.2060137

Cooper-Searle, S., Livesey, F., & Allwood, J. M. (2018). Why are material efficiency solutions a limited part of the climate policy agenda? An application of the Multiple Streams Framework to UK policy on CO2 emissions from cars. *Environmental Policy and Governance, 28*(1), 51–64. https://doi.org/10.1002/eet.1782

Derwort, P., Jager, N. W., & Newig, J. (2022). How to explain major policy change towards sustainability? Bringing together the multiple streams framework and the multilevel perspective on socio-technical transitions to explore the German "energiewende". *Policy Studies Journal, 50*(3), 671–699. https://doi.org/10.1111/psj.12428

Flinders, M., & Dimova, G. (2020, April 3). Bring in the experts: Blame deflection and the COVID-19 crisis. *British Policy and Politics at LSE.* http://eprints.lse.ac.uk/id/eprint/104501

Galanis, P., Vraka, I., Fragkou, D., Bilali, A., & Kaitelidou, D. (2021). Nurses' burnout and associated risk factors during the COVID-19 pandemic: A systematic review and meta-analysis. *Journal of Advanced Nursing, 77*(8), 3286–3302. https://doi.org/10.1111/jan.14839

Giese, K. K. (2020). Coronavirus disease 2019's shake-up of Telehealth policy: Application of Kingdon's multiple streams framework. *Journal for Nurse Practitioners, 16*(10), 768–770. https://doi.org/10.1016/j.nurpra.2020.08.015

Haktanir, A., Can, N., Seki, T., Kurnaz, M. F., & Dilmaç, B. (2022). Do we experience pandemic fatigue? current state, predictors, and prevention. *Current Psychology, 41*(10), 7314–7325. https://doi.org/10.1007/s12144-021-02397-w

Ho, K. K. L., & Chan, Y. T. (2021). Hong Kong's response to COVID-19: A glance to the control measures and their enforcement. *Social Transformations in Chinese Societies, 17*(2), 80–91. https://doi.org/10.1108/STICS-10-2020-0026

Hoefer, R. A. (2022). The multiple streams framework: Understanding and applying the problems, policies, and politics approach. *Journal of Policy Practice and Research, 3*(1), 1–5. https://doi.org/10.1007/s42972-022-00049-2

Hong Kong Special Administrative Region (HKSAR) Government. (2019). *CHP closely monitors cluster of pneumonia cases on mainland.* https://www.info.gov.hk/gia/general/202301/13/P2023011300407.htm?fontSize=1

Hong Kong Special Administrative Region (HKSAR) Government. (2020a, January 22). *CHP investigates highly suspected imported case of novel coronavirus infection.* https://www.info.gov.hk/gia/general/202001/22/P2020012200982.htm

Hong Kong Special Administrative Region (HKSAR) Government. (2020b, February 5). *CHP investigates three additional cases of novel coronavirus infection (2).* https://www.info.gov.hk/gia/general/202002/05/P2020020500690.htm

Hong Kong Special Administrative Region (HKSAR) Government. (2023a). *Coronavirus disease (COVID-19).* https://www.chp.gov.hk/en/healthtopics/content /24/102466.html

Hong Kong Special Administrative Region (HKSAR) Government. (2023b). *Elegislation – Prevention and control of disease (use of vaccines regulation).* https://www.elegislation.gov.hk/hk/cap599K

Hong Kong Special Administrative Region (HKSAR) Government. (2023c). *COVID-19 vaccination programme.* https://www.chp.gov.hk/en/features/106934.html

Hong Kong Special Administrative Region (HKSAR) Government. (2023d). *Statistics on government COVID-19 vaccination programme.* https://www.chp.gov.hk/en/ features/106989.html

Hong Kong Special Administrative Region (HKSAR) Government. (2023e, January 13). *Government adjusts evaluation criteria for COVID-19 nucleic acid test results.* https://www.info.gov.hk/gia/general/202301/13/P2023011300407.htm?fontSize=1

Hong Kong Special Administrative Region (HKSAR) Government. (2023f, January 19). *Government cancels arrangement of issuing isolation orders.* https://www.info .gov.hk/gia/general/202301/19/P2023011900678.htm

Hong Kong Special Administrative Region (HKSAR) Government. (2023g, February 28). *Government lifts all mandatory mask-wearing requirements.* https://www.info .gov.hk/gia/general/202302/28/P2023022800677.htm

Hong Kong Special Administrative Region (HKSAR) Government. (2023h, May 30). *Government lowers response level in relation to COVID-19 epidemic to Alert level.* https://www.info.gov.hk/gia/general/202305/30/P2023053000552.htm

Huang, J., Kwan, M.-P., & Kim, J. (2021). How culture and sociopolitical tensions might influence people's acceptance of COVID-19 control measures that use individual-level georeferenced data. *ISPRS International Journal of Geo-Information, 10*(7), 490. https://doi.org/10.3390/ijgi10070490

Hung, L. S. (2003). The SARS epidemic in Hong Kong: What lessons have we learned? *Journal of Royal Society of Medicine, 96*(8), 374–378. https://doi.org/10.1258/jrsm .96.8.374

Ioannidis, J. P. A., Zonta, F., & Levitt, M. (2023). Estimates of COVID-19 deaths in mainland China after abandoning zero COVID policy. *European Journal of Clinical Investigation, 52*(4), e13956. https://doi.org/10.1111/eci.13956

Kabir, M. J., Heidari, A., Honarvar, M. R., & Khatirnamani, Z. (2022). Analysis of electronic referral system agenda setting based on Kingdon multiple streams framework. *Payesh (Health Monitor), 21*(1), 25–33. http://payeshjournal.ir/article -1-1769-en.html

Kidd, M. R. (2020). Five principles for pandemic preparedness: Lessons from the Australian COVID-19 primary care response. *British Journal of General Practice, 70*(696), 316–317. https://doi.org/10.3399/bjgp20X710765

Kind, J., Maeschli, B., & Bruggmann, P. (2022). How to set the agenda for hepatitis C: A theory-driven policy analysis. *Health Research Policy and Systems, 20*(1), 20. https://doi.org/10.1186/s12961-022-00824-3

Kingdon, J. W. (2011). *Agendas, alternatives and public policies* (2nd ed.). Little Brown.

32   *Vincent T. S. Law and Ben Y. F. Fong*

Lau, S. S. S., Ho, C. C. Y., Pang, R. C. K., Su, S., Kwok, H., Fung, S., & Ho, R. C. (2022). COVID-19 burnout subject to the dynamic zero-COVID policy in Hong Kong: Development and psychometric evaluation of the COVID-19 burnout frequency scale. *Sustainability*, *14*(14), 8235. https://doi.org/10.3390/su14148235

Lavazza, A., & Farina, M. (2020). The role of experts in the Covid-19 pandemic and the limits of their epistemic authority in democracy. *Frontiers in Public Health*, *8*, 356. https://doi.org/10.3389/fpubh.2020.00356

Lee, S. H., Patel, P. C., & Phan, P. H. (2020). Are the self-employed more stressed? New evidence on an old question. *Journal of Small Business Management*, *61*(2), 513–539. https://doi.org/10.1080/00472778.2020.1796467

Loo, B. P. Y., Tsoi, K. H., Wong, P. P. Y., & Lai, P. C. (2021). Identification of superspreading environment under COVID-19 through human mobility data. *Scientific Reports*, *11*(1), 4699. https://doi.org/10.1038/s41598-021-84089-w

McGinty, E. E., Presskreischer, R., Han, H., & Barry, C. L. (2020). Psychological distress and loneliness reported by US adults in 2018 and April 2020. *JAMA*, *324*(1), 93–94. https://doi.org/10.1001/jama.2020.9740

Mishra, V., Seyedzenouzi, G., Almohtadi, A., Chowdhury, T., Khashkhusha, A., Axiaq, A., Wong, W. Y. E., & Harky, A. (2021). Health inequalities during COVID-19 and their effects on morbidity and mortality. *Journal of Healthcare Leadership*, *13*, 19–26. https://doi.org/10.2147/JHL.S270175

Moore, A., & MacKenzie, M. K. (2020). Policy making during crises: How diversity and disagreement can help manage the politics of expert advice. *BMJ*, m4039. https://www.bmj.com/content/371/bmj.m4039

Ratneswaren, A. (2020). The I in COVID: the importance of community and patient involvement in COVID-19 research. *Clinical Medicine Journal of Royal College of Physicians*, *20*, 10–12. https://doi.org/10.7861/CLINMED.2020-0173

Sapru, R. (2017). *Public policy: A contemporary perspective*. Sage.

Smith, V., & Cumming, J. (2017). Implementing pay-for-performance in primary health care: The role of institutional entrepreneurs. *Policy and Society*, *36*(4), 523–538. https://doi.org/10.1080/14494035.2017.1369617

Tee, M. L., Tee, C. A., Anlacan, J. P., Aligam, K. J. G., Reyes, P. W. C., Kuruchittham, V., & Ho, R. C. (2020). Psychological impact of COVID-19 pandemic in the Philippines. *Journal of Affective Disorders*, *277*, 379–391. https://doi.org/10.1016/j.jad.2020.08.043

Unlu, A., Tammi, T., & Hakkarainen, P. (2022). Policy windows for drug consumption rooms in Finland. *Nordic Studies on Alcohol and Drugs*, *39*(3), 205–224. https://doi.org/10.1177/14550725211069287

Valin, N., & Huitema, D. (2023). Experts as policy entrepreneurs: How knowledge can lead to radical environmental change. *Environmental Science & Policy*, *142*, 21–28. https://doi.org/10.1016/j.envsci.2023.01.013

Verlinghieri, E. (2020). Learning from the grassroots: A resourcefulness-based worldview for transport planning. *Transportation Research Part A: Policy and Practice*, *133*, 364–377. https://doi.org/10.1016/j.tra.2019.07.001

Vindegaard, N., & Benros, M. E. (2020). COVID-19 pandemic and mental health consequences: Systematic review of the current evidence. *Brain, Behavior, and Immunity*, *89*, 531–542. https://doi.org/10.1016/j.bbi.2020.05.048

Voo, T. C., Ballantyne, A., Jenn, N. C., Cowling, B. J., Xiao, J. Y., Chang, P. K., Kaur, S., Jenarun, G., Kumar, V., Lim, J. M. J., Tun, Z. M., Wong, N. C. B., & Tam, C. C.

(2021). Public perception of ethical issues related to COVID-19 control measures in Singapore, Hong Kong, and Malaysia: A cross-sectional survey. *MedRxiv*, 21252710. https://doi.org/10.1101/2021.03.01.21252710

Wang, S. S. Y. (2020). Journey to the east: COVID-19 lessons from the east. *Asia-Pacific Journal of Public Health*, *32*(8), 513–514. https://doi.org/10.1177/1010539520956442

World Health Organization (WHO). (2020a). *Risk communication and community engagement readiness and response to coronavirus disease (COVID-19): Interim guidance.* https://www.who.int/publications/i/item/risk-communication-and-community-engagement-readiness-and-initial-response-for-novel-coronaviruses

World Health Organization (WHO). (2020b). *Advice on the use of masks in the context of COVID-19: Interim guidance.* https://www.who.int/publications-detail/ advice-on-the-use-of-masks-in-the-community-during-home-care-and-in-healthcare-settings-in-the-context-of-the-novel-coronavirus-(2019- ncov)-outbreak

World Health Organization (WHO). (2023a). *Coronaviruses disease (COVID-19).* https://www.who.int/emergencies/diseases/novel-coronavirus-2019/question-and-answers-hub/q-a-detail/coronavirus-disease-covid-19

World Health Organization (WHO). (2023b). *WHO Coronavirus disease (COVID-19) Dashboard.* https://covid19.who.int/

World Health Organization (WHO). (2023c). *Statement on the fifteenth meeting of the IHR (2005) Emergency Committee on the COVID-19 pandemic.* https://www.who.int/news/item/05-05-2023-statement-on-the-fifteenth-meeting-of-the-international-health-regulations-(2005)-emergency-committee-regarding-the-coronavirus-disease-(covid-19)-pandemic

Yu, L., & Du, M. (2022). Social networking use, mental health, and quality of life of Hong Kong adolescents during the COVID-19 pandemic. *Frontiers in Public Health*, *10*, 1040169. https://doi.org/10.3389/fpubh.2022.1040169

Yuen, V. W. H. (2023). The efficacy of health experts' communication in inducing support for COVID-19 measures and effect on trustworthiness: A survey in Hong Kong. *Social Science & Medicine*, *317*, 115602. https://doi.org/10.1016/j.socscimed.2022.115602

Zhang, N., Chan, J. P. T., Wei, J., Dung, C.-H., Zhao, P. C., Lei, H., Su, B., Xue, P., Zhang, W. R., Xie, J. C., & Li, Y. G. (2021). Analysis of efficacy of intervention strategies for COVID-19 transmission: A case study of Hong Kong. *Environment International*, *156*, 106723. https://doi.org/10.1016/j.envint.2021.106723

3 Worldwide impacts on aged care during and after the COVID-19 pandemic

Tommy K. C. Ng and
Vincent T. S. Law

Abstract

The COVID-19 pandemic has had an enormous impact on all industries globally, particularly on aged care. The high morbidity and mortality of COVID-19 have had a negative impact on physical and psychological well-being for all individuals. Although restrictions and policies were implemented on aged care services, the mortality rate of COVID-19 in people aged 60 years or above is higher than that in other age groups. In aged care homes, older adults are living in a confined environment, resulting in remarkably high risks and rendering the execution of some preventive strategies difficult. Moreover, the deaths of COVID-19 in aged care homes vary among countries and cities. In this chapter, some restrictions implemented in aged care homes during the COVID-19 pandemic will be reviewed and the impact on aged care services during the pandemic will be evaluated from an international perspective. In addition, maintaining healthy ageing is important in aged care homes, and so the policy during and after the pandemic will be discussed.

Introduction

In December 2019, the coronavirus 2019 (COVID-19) was first reported in China. The World Health Organisation declared the COVID-19 infectious disease outbreak a public health emergency of international concern (PHEIC) on 30 January 2020 and a pandemic on 11 March 2020, in the light of more than 118,000 coronavirus cases spreading over 110 countries and the sustained risk of further global outbreak (World Health Organization, 2023a). The PHEIC was terminated by the World Health Organization on 5 May 2023 (World Health Organization, 2023b). As of 11 June 2023, there were more than 767 million confirmed cases of COVID-19 globally, including 6.9 million deaths (World Health Organization, 2023c). The COVID-19 pandemic has caused an enormous negative impact on global industries, including travel, hospitality, financial markets, and the healthcare sector (Ozili & Arun, 2023). The COVID-19 pandemic has caused a heavy burden

DOI: 10.4324/9781003436881-3

on the healthcare system because of the increase in the number of patients infected with COVID-19. During the COVID-19 pandemic, many countries implemented lockdown policies and enforced social-distancing restrictions to limit the spread of COVID-19 in the community. The restrictions caused a negative impact on physical and psychological well-being for all individuals because most of them were not able to have enough physical activity and a normal social lifestyle. In addition, most of the medical resources were switched to combat the pandemic, so non-COVID-19 care was suspended or cancelled (Arsenault et al., 2022). The reduction of essential healthcare services during the COVID-19 pandemic had affected different healthcare services (Josephson & Gillombardo, 2023; Pirozzolo et al., 2023; Thompson et al., 2020).

Older adults were one of the most vulnerable groups during the COVID-19 pandemic (Prendki et al., 2022; Shahid et al., 2020). The incidence and mortality rate of COVID-19 among older adults is found to be higher than the young generation (O'Driscoll et al., 2021; Niessen et al., 2022). The mortality rate of COVID-19 in people aged 60 years or above is higher than that in other age groups (Wong et al., 2023). According to the World Health Organization (2023d), seven out of ten COVID-19 deaths were in older adults aged 65 years old and above (from 31 December 2019 to 19 June 2023). Older adults are at higher risk of contracting COVID-19 and developing severe illness if they contract the disease (Rana, 2023). Insufficient personal protective equipment at aged homes at the beginning of the pandemic was reported and it increased the spread of COVID-19 at aged homes (ECDC Public Health Emergency Team et al., 2020). Restrictions of aged homes led to other challenges of caring for older adults. The mental health of the older adults was affected due to the social isolation during the pandemic. Therefore, those living in aged care homes during the COVID-19 pandemic were under higher risk of getting infected with COVID-19. In this chapter, the impacts on aged care during the COVID-19 pandemic in Australia, Hong Kong, and the UK will be reviewed. Through the lessons from the COVID-19 pandemic, the future of aged care will be discussed.

Situation of aged care in the selected regions during the COVID-19 pandemic

Australia

In Australia, 6% of those over 65 years of age are receiving residential aged care services (Department of Health and Aged Care, 2022). The COVID-19 pandemic had a significant impact on the aged care in Australia. Approximately one-third of the fatal cases of COVID-19 were the residents living in residential aged care facilities (Australian Bureau of Statistics, 2023; Department of Health and Aged Care, 2023). The risk of residents living in aged care settings contracting COVID-19 was 1.27 times higher than the general population (Quigley et al., 2022). The first outbreak of a residential aged care home was at Newmarch House, which is located in western Sydney (McCracken, 2021; Webb, 2023). The outbreak at Newmarch House was the largest outbreak at the early stage of the pandemic in Australia. The Independent Review commissioned by the Commonwealth Department of Health had reviewed the outbreak at Newmarch House and highlighted some areas that needed to be addressed, such as lack of clarity of the relationships among government health agencies, shortage of staff due to COVID-19 infection or quarantine, and infection control in the residential aged care home (Department of Health and Aged Care, 2020). Twyford (2023) summarised that the privatisation of residential aged care homes in Australia led to a significant impact on aged care during the COVID-19 pandemic. Since more than half of the residential aged care homes were operated by not-for-profit entities, it had problems with the operations management of private residential aged care homes. The residents and staff were trapped in Newmarch House because of the diverse responsibilities of government health agencies. Eventually, 17 out of 37 residents at Newmarch House died directly attributed to COVID-19. Nevertheless, the early lockdown introduced by the Australian government had successfully reduced the impact of COVID-19 in the residential aged care home (Chan et al., 2021).

Hong Kong

The Hong Kong population, claiming the highest life expectancy in the world is ageing rapidly. The demands of the aged care services are rising. About one-tenth of older adults aged 80 years and above live in homes for the elderly (Census and Statistics Department, 2023a). The pandemic had caused severe impacts on older adults living in residential care home for the elderly. The fifth wave of the COVID-19 in Hong Kong, from 31 December 2021 to 29 January 2023, has claimed more than 13,000 lives, while over 95% of the deceased were older adults aged 60 years or above (Centre for Health Protection, 2023). More than 40% of the deceased were the residents of the residential care home, and it shows that the COVID-19 pandemic affected the aged care service in Hong Kong. The confined living space of the residential care home is one of the factors causing a high infection rate of COVID-19 among older adults. Besides, the design of most of the elderly care homes is an open area on a single floor, so it increases the cross-contamination of highly transmissible COVID-19 in the residential care home for the elderly (Das, 2022). At the beginning of the fifth wave of the COVID-19 pandemic, there were many positive cases, and lots of patients rushed to the Accident and Emergency Departments of public hospitals. Lots of patients, most of them being older adults, were left in the open areas outside the Accident and Emergency Departments of public hospitals in the cold and rainy weather because the hospitals did not have enough space and manpower to handle the sudden surge of positive cases (Fong, 2022).

United Kingdom

The aged care in the United Kingdom was affected by the COVID-19 pandemic as well. There were over 210,000 deaths involving COVID-19 and more than 45,000 deaths in care homes from March 2020 to December 2022 (Office for National Statistics, 2023a, 2023b). With nationwide lockdown in March 2020, London still experienced large and sustained outbreaks in many care homes (Ladhani et al., 2020). The potential sources of the infection in the care homes included the care home staff, residents returning to care homes from hospitals, new residents, and visitors to the care homes (Ladhani et al., 2020). More than half of the staff and residents in the care homes had been asymptomatic (Marossy et al., 2021). The situation of under-detection of COVID-19 in care homes might reduce the effectiveness of infection control measures. Besides, new admissions to the care homes and poor compliance with disease control measures were associated with the outbreaks among staff and residents of care homes (Shallcross et al., 2021).

Impact on aged care during the COVID-19 pandemic

The COVID-19 pandemic has led to heavy burden and significant impact on aged care worldwide. Governments had to implement different measures for the aged care, such as visitor restrictions, adoption of a closed-loop system, social distancing, and vaccination. Due to the strict restrictions and measures, some innovative healthcare services have emerged, such as telehealth and remote monitoring. Those digital health services can be recognised as a positive impact on aged care.

Visitor restrictions

As mentioned above, the COVID-19 outbreaks in aged care homes could be caused by the staff and visitors who were already infected outside of the care homes. Therefore, visitor restrictions were implemented in most of the aged care homes. Restrictions on visitor access and social distancing were implemented in the residential aged care facilities in Australia and Hong Kong at the early stage of the pandemic (Lum et al., 2020; Murray et al., 2023). The stringent policy on visiting older adults in aged care homes did not allow both family members of the older adults and volunteers to have face-to-face visits. In the United Kingdom, there were no compulsory regulations to forbid face-to-face visits to the aged care homes, but some aged care homes did not allow visitors to visit the older adults (Chan et al., 2021). The stringent visitation rules had contributed to the changes in mental health of the older adults. In Australia, the older adults living in residential aged care had shown poor mental health, increased loneliness, and increased stress and anxiety because of the restrictions on visitation and outings, as well as concerns for the safety of family or friends (Brydon et al., 2022). In Hong Kong, the older adults experienced increased loneliness, anxiety, and insomnia after the onset of the COVID-19 pandemic (Wong et al., 2020). The older adults could not have face-to-face interactions with their relatives and friends. Although older adults might use electronic means to contact and communicate with others, it could not reduce the risk of mental health deterioration (Litwin & Levinsky, 2022). The visitation restrictions in aged care homes might cause social isolation that could affect the mental health status of older adults.

Infection prevention and control

Infection prevention and control is vital for limiting the spread of COVID-19 in healthcare settings. Nevertheless, the changeable and transforming restrictions have forced hospitals and aged care homes to adopt different levels of infection prevention and control measures. The transformational infection prevention and control measures have caused increased workloads for the healthcare workers working in aged care homes in Hong Kong (Lai et al., 2022). Additional care workloads were needed among healthcare workers because the care was originally shared by the family members. In addition, the demand for personal protective equipment was extremely high for hospitals and aged care homes during the COVID-19 pandemic. A worldwide shortage of personal protective equipment caused a significant impact on the healthcare sector. The frontline healthcare workers are the most vulnerable groups during the COVID-19 pandemic, so the shortage of personal protective equipment caused them an exhausting working environment. The healthcare workers might need to wear personal protective equipment the whole day and, therefore, experienced some unexpected discomfort and adverse events, including dermatitis, allergy, overheating, dehydration, and breathlessness (Chen et al., 2021; Galanis et al., 2021). Apart from a shortage of protective equipment, a lack of staff training on infection prevention and control in the residential aged care facilities was one of the underlying factors for the transmission of COVID-19 in the aged care homes.

Manpower shortage

The shortage of workforce in aged care is a critical and challenging issue worldwide. Understaffing in the aged care homes can lead to older adults living in aged care homes being at higher risk of potential adverse events, such as falls and missing the prime time for first aid (Li & Shi, 2022). Manpower shortage was already a serious problem before the COVID-19 pandemic and the pandemic had deepened the impact of manpower shortage in aged care.

Increased workload and working hours of healthcare workers were identified during the pandemic (Doleman et al., 2023). The ratio of healthcare providers and nurses increased during the pandemic. If the nursing staff and other healthcare providers working in aged care homes contracted COVID-19, they had to isolate from the aged care home and the manpower could become more intense. Therefore, at least half of the manpower in care homes were unable to work because of the infection of COVID-19 (Lam, 2022). With insufficient manpower, the quality of care to older adults in aged care homes might be reduced. Besides, the staff could feel fatigued and frustrated due to the shortage of manpower during the pandemic (Brydon et al., 2022). Manpower shortage in aged care was negatively affected during the COVID-19 pandemic.

Vaccination roll-out

Vaccination is one of the methods to provide protection against COVID-19. Many countries competed to purchase vaccines for protecting citizens. However, vaccine hesitancy among older adults is a great concern in aged care. Delay, refusal, and unwillingness of COVID-19 vaccine can be defined as vaccine hesitancy. The uptake rates of COVID-19 vaccine among Hong Kong older adults were lower than those in the United Kingdom and Singapore (Yuen et al., 2023). Although the vaccination was free of charge and the Hong Kong government restricted the entering into catering business premises, it did not motivate older adults to uptake the vaccine. Lack of support from healthcare professionals, family, and government was one of the reasons explaining older adults' delay or refusal for COVID-19 vaccination (Yuen et al., 2023). In Australia, the priority of COVID-19 vaccination included frontline healthcare workers and older adults. The Australian older adults were more likely to accept COVID-19 vaccination (Bullivant et al., 2023). Some factors influencing COVID-19 vaccination decisions among older adults included perceived safety, effectiveness, and benefits of the COVID-19 vaccine, perceived COVID-19 disease risk, and financial cost of doctor consultations on vaccination. In the United Kingdom, almost three-quarters of the older adults had no concerns about the COVID-19 vaccines, but some of them worried about the potential vaccine side effects and efficacy (Gallant et al., 2021). The factors affecting vaccine uptake among older adults were mainly about the safety and efficacy of the vaccines.

Adoption of telecommunication and telehealth

Most of the aged care homes adopted visitor restrictions during the COVID-19 pandemic so that family members and friends could not visit the older adults, while they could not meet others face to face. Therefore, electronic devices for communication and medical consultation were widely used during the pandemic. The coverage of the Internet is growing due to technological advancement so older adults are more likely to access the Internet. Although Internet use among older adults is increasing, older adults still lag far behind the younger generation (Hunsaker & Hargittai, 2018). In Hong Kong, the percentage of persons aged 65 years or above who had used the Internet increased from 44.0% in 2016 to 81.8% in 2022 (Census and Statistics Department, 2019, 2023b). In the United Kingdom, there were 21.5% of older adults aged 65 to 74 years and 56.5% of older adults aged 75 years or above who had never used the Internet in 2016, and the figures decreased to 11.4% for age 65 to 74 years and 38.8% for age 75 years or above in 2020 (Office for National Statistics, 2021). During the pandemic, the largest increase in use was of chat software among older adults (Nimrod, 2020). The statistics show that the pandemic facilitated the change in Internet use among older adults worldwide. Furthermore, the adoption and development of telehealth was growing dramatically in aged care. Some researchers have found significant increases in the use of telehealth among older adults during the COVID-19 pandemic (Choi et al., 2022; Qin, 2022). Using telehealth can overcome the restrictions in aged care and deliver quality and safe healthcare services to older adults. Telehealth is helpful to older adults in many aspects, such as reducing negative emotions, overcoming delayed healthcare due to COVID-19 concerns, and having feasible and flexible healthcare services (Hao et al., 2023).

Impact on aged care after the COVID-19 pandemic

Improving staffing levels and infection prevention and control

The staffing level in aged care was insufficient during the pandemic. The infected healthcare workers were isolated from the aged care homes, so fewer manpower were able to provide care for the older adults. The use of temporary staff in aged care homes is not a long-term solution to staffing levels after the pandemic. It is important that governments review the staffing levels of aged care homes and consider providing aged care training and support for the healthcare workers. Additionally, some researchers revealed that most of the aged care homes had implemented infection prevention and control programmes before the pandemic (Lee et al., 2019; Mitchell et al., 2019). However, the pandemic had a significant impact on aged care. Therefore, aged care homes have integrated updated infection prevention and control for daily care after the COVID-19 pandemic.

Digital aged care

The strict restrictions, such as social distancing and visitor restrictions, and insufficient manpower during the COVID-19 pandemic constituted some huge challenges in aged care. To tackle the problems and challenges encountered, many countries have adopted and developed digital aged care. Telehealth must be the most widely used healthcare service during the

COVID-19 pandemic. It can reduce the risk of infection and improve the accessibility of healthcare services for older adults because the medical consultation can be delivered remotely. Positive impacts of telehealth on older adults were also reported, including less loneliness and improved quality of life (Raja et al., 2021). Nevertheless, difficulties in remembering the instructions were reported as one of the barriers when using telehealth by older adults (Raja et al., 2021). Therefore, the staff in the aged care home must be well trained to use telehealth in order to help the older adults use telehealth easily. Apart from the provision of training for staff, the usability of the telehealth is also vital for the development of telehealth in aged care homes. Older adults would feel frustrated when the usability of the telehealth platform was lacking interpretation (Zhang et al., 2022). With more frustration on the use of telehealth, older adults would not be likely to continue to use telehealth in the future. Hence, the usability of the telehealth platform has to be clear and simple.

Concluding Remarks

The COVID-19 pandemic has significantly affected healthcare across the world. The rapid spread of COVID-19 has caught everyone off guard. More than 80% of the total COVID-19 deaths were people aged 60 years or above, so the older adults are the most vulnerable group during the pandemic (Wong et al., 2023). The impact on aged care during the COVID-19 pandemic was enormous, not only because of the deaths incurred by COVID-19 but also the governments' response on aged care during the pandemic. The initial policy in Australia, which was an earlier national lockdown policy, earlier visitation restriction in aged care homes, and availability of viral testing, have contributed to fewer lives lost in the aged care sector compared to the United Kingdom (Chan et al., 2021). In Hong Kong, the border restrictions, quarantine, isolation, and social-distancing measures have effectively reduced the confirmed cases over the second and third waves of the pandemic, but the low vaccination rate among people aged over 80 years caused more deaths from COVID-19 in the older adults (Chen et al., 2022). The government responses and interventions to combat COVID-19 have contributed to the consequences of the COVID-19 pandemic among older adults. Additionally, vaccine hesitancy among older adults affected the uptake of vaccination. Chen et al. (2022) concluded that more older adults being fully vaccinated is the best strategy for reducing deaths from COVID-19. The government should reconsider the past strategies of vaccination promotion because the promotion of vaccination is vital for combating the pandemic in the future.

The future development and adoption of telehealth is essential to aged care. Although there were many challenges and impacts on aged care during the COVID-19 pandemic, the pandemic has contributed to the development and implementation of new care delivery models. The use of telehealth was implemented in aged care homes to reduce face-to-face medical consultations and decrease transmission of disease. The barriers and challenges of using telehealth have been investigated by many researchers, so future telehealth platforms should have fewer barriers. In addition, governments should take a leading role in promoting the use of telehealth in aged care in order to improve the accessibility of healthcare services and reduce the burden on public healthcare services. Apart from the provision of training in the use of telehealth, the support of hardware and software for telehealth is fundamental in aged care homes.

References

Arsenault, C., Gage, A., Kim, M. K., Kapoor, N. R., Akweongo, P., Amponsah, F., ... Kruk, M. E. (2022). COVID-19 and resilience of healthcare systems in ten countries. *Nature Medicine, 28*(6), 1314–1324. https://doi.org/10.1038/s41591-022-01750-1

Australian Bureau of Statistics. (2023). *COVID-19 Mortality in Australia: Deaths registered until 30 April 2023*. https://www.abs.gov.au/articles/covid-19-mortality -australia-deaths-registered-until-30-april-2023

Brydon, A., Bhar, S., Doyle, C., Batchelor, F., Lovelock, H., Almond, H., ... Wuthrich, V. (2022). National survey on the impact of COVID-19 on the mental health of Australian residential aged care residents and staff. *Clinical Gerontologist, 45*(1), 58–70. https://doi.org/10.1080/07317115.2021.1985671

Bullivant, B., Bolsewicz, K. T., King, C., & Steffens, M. S. (2023). COVID-19 vaccination acceptance among older adults: A qualitative study in New South Wales, Australia. *Public Health in Practice, 5*, 100349. https://doi.org/10.1016/j .puhip.2022.100349

Census and Statistics Department. (2019). *Thematic household survey report - Report no. 67 - Information technology usage and penetration*. https://www.censtatd.gov .hk/en/data/stat_report/product/B1130201/att/B11302672019XXXXB0100.pdf

Census and Statistics Department. (2023a). *Hong Kong 2016 population by-census - Thematic report: Older persons*. https://www.censtatd.gov.hk/en/data/stat_report/ product/B1120105/att/B11201052016XXXXB0100.pdf

Census and Statistics Department. (2023b). *Thematic household survey report - Report no. 77 - Information technology usage and penetration*. https://www.censtatd.gov .hk/en/data/stat_report/product/B1130201/att/B11302772023XXXXB0100.pdf

Centre for Health Protection. (2023). *Archive of statistics on provisional analysis on reported death cases*. https://www.coronavirus.gov.hk/pdf/death_analysis/death _analysis_20230129.pdf

Chan, D. K. Y., Mclaws, M. L., & Forsyth, D. R. (2021). COVID-19 in aged care homes: A comparison of effects initial government policies had in the UK (primarily focussing on England) and Australia during the first wave. *International Journal for Quality in Health Care, 33*(1), mzab033. https://doi.org/10.1093/intqhc/mzab033

Chen, C. W., So, M. K., & Liu, F. C. (2022). Assessing government policies' impact on the COVID-19 pandemic and elderly deaths in East Asia. *Epidemiology and Infection, 150*, e161. https://doi.org/10.1017/S0950268822001388

44   *Tommy K. C. Ng and Vincent T. S. Law*

Chen, F., Zang, Y., Liu, Y., Wang, X., & Lin, X. (2021). Dispatched nurses' experience of wearing full gear personal protective equipment to care for COVID-19 patients in China—A descriptive qualitative study. *Journal of Clinical Nursing, 30*(13–14), 2001–2014. https://doi.org/10.1111/jocn.15753

Choi, N. G., DiNitto, D. M., Marti, C. N., & Choi, B. Y. (2022). Telehealth use among older adults during COVID-19: Associations with sociodemographic and health characteristics, technology device ownership, and technology learning. *Journal of Applied Gerontology, 41*(3), 600–609. https://doi.org/10.1177/07334648211047347

Das, M. (2022). COVID-19 and the elderlies: How safe are Hong Kong's care homes? *Frontiers in Public Health, 10*, 883472. https://doi.org/10.3389/fpubh.2022.883472

Department of Health and Aged Care. (2020). *Newmarch house COVID-19 outbreak independent review – Final report*. https://www.health.gov.au/sites/default/files/documents/2020/08/coronavirus-covid-19-newmarch-house-covid-19-outbreak-independent-review-newmarch-house-covid-19-outbreak-independent-review-final-report.pdf

Department of Health and Aged Care. (2022). *2021–22 report on the operation of the aged care act 1997*. https://www.gen-agedcaredata.gov.au/www_aihwgen/media/ROACA/22506-Health-and-Aged-Care-ROACA-2021-22-Web_May2023.pdf

Department of Health and Aged Care. (2023). *COVID-19 outbreaks in Australian residential aged care facilities – 28 April 2023*. https://www.health.gov.au/sites/default/files/2023-04/covid-19-outbreaks-in-australian-residential-aged-care-facilities-28-april-2023.pdf

Doleman, G., De Leo, A., & Bloxsome, D. (2023). The impact of pandemics on healthcare providers' workloads: A scoping review. *Journal of Advanced Nursing.* https://doi.org/10.1111/jan.15690

ECDC Public Health Emergency Team, Danis, K., Fontenau, L., Georges, S., Daniau, C., & Bernard-Stoecklin, S., Domegan, L., ... &Schneider, E. (2020). High impact of COVID-19 in long-term care facilities,suggestion for monitoring in the EU/EEA, May 2020. *Eurosurveillance, 25*(22), 2000956. https://doi.org/10.2807/1560-7917.ES.2020.25.22.2000956

Fong, B. Y. F. (2022). *Live old and let "die"*. https://www.springernature.com/gp/researchers/the-source/blog/blogposts-communicating-research/live-old-and-let-die/23186318

Galanis, P., Vraka, I., Fragkou, D., Bilali, A., & Kaitelidou, D. (2021). Impact of personal protective equipment use on health care workers' physical health during the COVID-19 pandemic: A systematic review and meta-analysis. *American Journal of Infection Control, 49*(10), 1305–1315. https://doi.org/10.1016/j.ajic.2021.04.084

Gallant, A. J., Nicholls, L. A. B., Rasmussen, S., Cogan, N., Young, D., & Williams, L. (2021). Changes in attitudes to vaccination as a result of the COVID-19 pandemic: A longitudinal study of older adults in the UK. *PLoS One, 16*(12), e0261844. https://doi.org/10.1371/journal.pone.0261844

Hao, X., Qin, Y., Lv, M., Zhao, X., Wu, S., & Li, K. (2023). Effectiveness of Telehealth interventions on psychological outcomes and quality of life in community adults during the COVID-19 pandemic: A systematic review and meta-analysis. *International Journal of Mental Health Nursing, 32*(4), 979–1007. https://doi.org/10.1111/inm.13126

Hunsaker, A., & Hargittai, E. (2018). A review of Internet use among older adults. *New Media and Society, 20*(10), 3937–3954. https://doi.org/10.1177/1461444818787348

Josephson, R. A., & Gillombardo, C. B. (2023). Cardiovascular services in Covid-19-Impact of the pandemic and lessons learned. *Progress in Cardiovascular Diseases*, *76*, 12–19. https://doi.org/10.1016/j.pcad.2023.01.005

Ladhani, S. N., Chow, J. Y., Janarthanan, R., Fok, J., Crawley-Boevey, E., Vusirikala, A., ... Zambon, M. (2020). Investigation of SARS-CoV-2 outbreaks in six care homes in London, April 2020. *eClinicalMedicine*, *26*, 100533. https://doi.org/10.1016/j.eclinm.2020.100533

Lai, V. S. K., Yau, S. Y., Lee, L. Y. K., Li, B. S. Y., Law, S. S. P., & Huang, S. (2022). Caring for older people during and beyond the COVID-19 pandemic: Experiences of residential health care workers. *International Journal of Environmental Research and Public Health*, *19*(22), 15287. https://doi.org/10.3390/ijerph192215287

Lam, N. (2022, March 1). Coronavirus: 56 per cent of Hong Kong care homes have infections, city to bring in 1,000 temporary workers from mainland China. *South China Morning Post*. https://www.scmp.com/news/hong-kong/health-environment/article/3168767/coronavirus-hong-kong-56-cent-care-homes-have

Lee, M. H., Lee, G. A., Lee, S. H., & Park, Y. H. (2019). Effectiveness and core components of infection prevention and control programmes in long-term care facilities: A systematic review. *Journal of Hospital Infection*, *102*(4), 377–393. https://doi.org/10.1016/j.jhin.2019.02.008

Li, C., & Shi, C. (2022). Adverse events and risk management in residential aged care facilities: A cross-sectional study in Hunan, China. *Risk Management and Healthcare Policy*, *15*, 529–542. https://doi.org/10.2147/RMHP.S351821

Litwin, H., & Levinsky, M. (2022). Social networks and mental health change in older adults after the Covid-19 outbreak. *Aging and Mental Health*, *26*(5), 925–931. https://doi.org/10.1080/13607863.2021.1902468

Lum, T., Shi, C., Wong, G., & Wong, K. (2020). COVID-19 and long-term care policy for older people in Hong Kong. *Journal of Aging and Social Policy*, *32*(4–5), 373–379. https://doi.org/10.1080/08959420.2020.1773192

Marossy, A., Rakowicz, S., Bhan, A., Noon, S., Rees, A., Virk, M., ... Zuckerman, M. (2021). A study of universal severe acute respiratory syndrome coronavirus 2 RNA testing among residents and staff in a large group of care homes in South London. *The Journal of Infectious Diseases*, *223*(3), 381–388. https://doi.org/10.1093/infdis/jiaa565

McCracken, K. (2021). COVID-19: The Australian experience. In R. Akhtar (Ed.), *Coronavirus (COVID-19) outbreaks, environment and human behaviour* (pp. 173–192). Springer. https://doi.org/10.1007/978-3-030-68120-3_11

Mitchell, B. G., Shaban, R. Z., MacBeth, D., & Russo, P. (2019). Organisation and governance of infection prevention and control in Australian residential aged care facilities: A national survey. *Infection, Disease and Health*, *24*(4), 187–193. https://doi.org/10.1016/j.idh.2019.04.004

Murray, C. M., Milanese, S., Guerin, M., Bilton, R., Baldock, K. L., & Parfitt, G. (2023). Exploring what matters to residents of Australian aged care facilities with the happy Life Index: Comparison of qualitative responses between pre-and mid-Covid-19 pandemic time points. *Quality of Life Research*, *32*(8), 2247–2257. https://doi.org/10.1007/s11136-023-03387-0

Niessen, A., Teirlinck, A. C., McDonald, S. A., van der Hoek, W., van Gageldonk-Lafeber, R., RIVM COVID-19 Epidemiology, Surveillance Group, & Knol, M. J. (2022). Sex differences in COVID-19 mortality in the Netherlands. *Infection*, *50*(3), 709–717. https://doi.org/10.1007/s15010-021-01744-0

Nimrod, G. (2020). Changes in internet use when coping with stress: Older adults during the COVID-19 pandemic. *American Journal of Geriatric Psychiatry, 28*(10), 1020–1024. https://doi.org/10.1016/j.jagp.2020.07.010

O'Driscoll, M., Ribeiro Dos Santos, G., Wang, L., Cummings, D. A., Azman, A. S., Paireau, J., ... Salje, H. (2021). Age-specific mortality and immunity patterns of SARS-CoV-2. *Nature, 590*(7844), 140–145. https://doi.org/10.1038/s41586-020-2918-0

Office for National Statistics. (2021). *Internet users*. https://www.ons.gov.uk/businessindustryandtrade/itandinternetindustry/datasets/internetusers

Office for National Statistics. (2023a). *Deaths in care homes, UK*. https://www.ons.gov.uk/peoplepopulationandcommunity/healthandsocialcare/socialcare/datasets/deathsincarehomesuk

Office for National Statistics. (2023b). *Deaths involving coronavirus (COVID-19) by month of registration, UK*. https://www.ons.gov.uk/peoplepopulationandcommunity/birthsdeathsandmarriages/deaths/datasets/deathsinvolvingcovid19bymonthofregistrationuk

Ozili, P. K., & Arun, T. (2023). Spillover of COVID-19: Impact on the global economy. In U. Akkucuk (Ed.), *Managing inflation and supply chain disruptions in the global economy* (pp. 41–61). IGI Global. https://doi.org/10.4018/978-1-6684-5876-1.ch004

Pirozzolo, G., Quoc, B. R., Vignotto, C., Baiano, L., Piangerelli, A., Peluso, C., ... Recordare, A. G. (2023). The impact of COVID-19 pandemic on access to medical services and its consequences on emergency surgery. *Frontiers in Surgery, 10*, 1059517. https://doi.org/10.3389/fsurg.2023.1059517

Prendki, V., Tiseo, G., Falcone, M., & ESCMID Study Group for Infections in the Elderly (ESGIE) (2022). Caring for older adults during the COVID-19 pandemic. *Clinical Microbiology and Infection, 28*(6), 785–791. https://doi.org/10.1016/j.cmi.2022.02.040

Public, E. C. D. C., Health Emergency Team, Danis, K., Fonteneau, L., Georges, S., Daniau, C., Bernard-Stoecklin, S., Domegan, L., ... Schneider, E. (2020). High impact of COVID-19 in long-term care facilities, suggestion for monitoring in the EU/EEA, May 2020. *Eurosurveillance, 25*(22), 2000956. https://doi.org/10.2807/1560-7917.ES.2020.25.22.2000956

Qin, W. (2022). Technology learning and the adoption of Telehealth among community-dwelling older adults during the COVID-19 outbreak. *Journal of Applied Gerontology, 41*(7), 1651–1656. https://doi.org/10.1177/07334648221085473

Quigley, A., Stone, H., Nguyen, P. Y., Chughtai, A. A., & MacIntyre, C. R. (2022). COVID-19 outbreaks in aged-care facilities in Australia. *Influenza and Other Respiratory Viruses, 16*(3), 429–437. https://doi.org/10.1111/irv.12942

Raja, M., Bjerkan, J., Kymre, I. G., Galvin, K. T., & Uhrenfeldt, L. (2021). Telehealth and digital developments in society that persons 75 years and older in European countries have been part of: A scoping review. *BMC Health Services Research, 21*(1), 1–15. https://doi.org/10.1186/s12913-021-07154-0

Rana, R. (2023). Impact of Covid-19 on older population: Review of the initial phase. In M. K. Shankardass (Ed.), *Handbook on COVID-19 pandemic and older persons* (pp. 13–19). Springer. https://doi.org/10.1007/978-981-99-1467-8_2

Shahid, Z., Kalayanamitra, R., McClafferty, B., Kepko, D., Ramgobin, D., Patel, R., ... Jain, R. (2020). COVID-19 and older adults: What we know. *Journal of the American Geriatrics Society, 68*(5), 926–929. https://doi.org/10.1111/jgs.16472

Shallcross, L., Burke, D., Abbott, O., Donaldson, A., Hallatt, G., Hayward, A., ... Thorne, S. (2021). Factors associated with SARS-CoV-2 infection and outbreaks in long-term care facilities in England: A national cross-sectional survey. *Lancet Healthy Longevity*, *2*(3), e129–e142. https://doi.org/10.1016/S2666-7568(20)30065-9

Thompson, D. C., Barbu, M. G., Beiu, C., Popa, L. G., Mihai, M. M., Berteanu, M., & Popescu, M. N. (2020). The impact of COVID-19 pandemic on long-term care facilities worldwide: An overview on international issues. *BioMed Research International*, *2020*, 8870249. https://doi.org/10.1155/2020/8870249

Twyford, E. J. (2023). Crisis accountability and aged "care" during COVID-19. *Meditari Accountancy Research*, *31*(1), 27–51. https://doi.org/10.1108/MEDAR-05-2021-1296

Webb, E. O. (2023). Older Australians during the COVID-19 pandemic: Experiences and responses. In M. K. Shankardass (Ed.), *Handbook on COVID-19 pandemic and older persons* (pp. 257–275). Springer. https://doi.org/10.1007/978-981-99-1467-8_17

Wong, M. K., Brooks, D. J., Ikejezie, J., Gacic-Dobo, M., Dumolard, L., Nedelec, Y., ... Van Kerkhove, M. D. (2023). COVID-19 mortality and progress toward vaccinating older adults—World Health Organization, worldwide, 2020–2022. *Morbidity and Mortality Weekly Report*, *72*(5), 113–118. https://doi.org/10.15585/mmwr.mm7205a1

Wong, S. Y. S., Zhang, D., Sit, R. W. S., Yip, B. H. K., Chung, R. Y. N., Wong, C. K. M., ... Mercer, S. W. (2020). Impact of COVID-19 on loneliness, mental health, and health service utilisation: A prospective cohort study of older adults with multimorbidity in primary care. *British Journal of General Practice*, *70*(700), e817–e824. https://doi.org/10.3399/bjgp20X713021

World Health Organization. (2023a). *Timeline: WHO's COVID-19 response*. https://www.who.int/emergencies/diseases/novel-coronavirus-2019/interactive-timeline

World Health Organization. (2023b). *Statement on the fifteenth meeting of the IHR (2005). Emergency committee on the COVID-19 pandemic*. https://www.who.int/news/item/05-05-2023-statement-on-the-fifteenth-meeting-of-the-international-health-regulations-(2005)-emergency-committee-regarding-the-coronavirus-disease-(covid-19)-pandemic

World Health Organization. (2023c). *Weekly epidemiological update on COVID-19 −15 June 2023*. https://www.who.int/docs/default-source/coronaviruse/situation-reports/20230615_weekly_epi_update_147.pdf?sfvrsn=d7d5a1f_3&download=true

World Health Organization. (2023d). *WHO COVID-19 detailed surveillance data dashboard*. https://app.powerbi.com/view?r=eyJrIjoiYWRiZWVkNWUtNmM0Ni00MDAwLTljYWMtN2EwNTM3YjQzYmRmIiwidCI6ImY2MTBjMGI3LWJkMjQtNGIzOS04MTBiLTNkYzI4MGFmYjU5MCIsImMiOjh9

Yuan, J., Lam, W. W. T., Xiao, J., Ni, M. Y., Cowling, B. J., & Liao, Q. (2023). Why do Chinese older adults in Hong Kong delay or refuse COVID-19 vaccination? A qualitative study based on grounded theory. *The Journals of Gerontology: Series B*, *78*(4), 736–748. https://doi.org/10.1093/geronb/gbac184

Zhang, Z., Henley, T., Schiaffino, M., Wiese, J., Sachs, D., Migliaccio, J., & Huh-Yoo, J. (2022). Older adults' perceptions of community-based Telehealth wellness programs: A qualitative study. *Informatics for Health and Social Care*, *47*(4), 361–372. https://doi.org/10.1080/17538157.2021.2006198

4 Experience of aged care from Asia-Pacific during the COVID-19 pandemic

Carina Y. H. Lam and Wang-Kin Chiu

Abstract

COVID-19 is a highly contagious and potentially fatal disease, especially among the immune-compromised population. Since 2020, numerous measures have been implemented among the community to identify and isolate the infected population, yet the death of the aged population related to the pandemic has increased along with the progression of COVID-19. Across the Asia-Pacific region, the aged care services have undergone big changes in areas of infection, including identification and management, isolation of infected individuals, family visits, and daily activity planning, to enhance infection control. Meanwhile, the effectiveness of these measures has varied due to the continuous mutation of the COVID-19 virus, the quality of healthcare services, and the average education level in different countries. Pandemic management measures targeting the aged population have created a huge challenge in maintaining the physical, social, and mental well-being of the aged care residents, and the resources management of the aged care facilities, which have contributed to an increased risk of other illnesses. Governments should work closely with each other to share knowledge and technology targeting to allocate resources efficiently and minimise the health and socioeconomic consequences of the pandemic, thus the impact on the quality of life of their residents. This chapter aims to review and report the experience of aged care services in Hong Kong and summarise the similar measures in other Asia-Pacific countries such as Singapore and Thailand under the COVID-19 pandemic.

Introduction

In 2019, the human-infected cases of COVID-19 were first reported by officials in China and the novel coronavirus causing the disease was named as the severe acute respiratory syndrome coronavirus-2, SARS-CoV-2, 2019-nCoV (Yuki et al., 2020). Studies have shown that older people have a higher mortality rate than younger people for this disease (Dadras et al., 2022). COVID-19 is a highly contagious disease transmitted through close contact,

DOI: 10.4324/9781003436881-4

with relevant data and findings showing that more than 75% of infected individuals in the same family got the virus from the same source. Older adults living in nursing homes, whose living environment is usually highly dense and whose immune function is generally weaker due to ageing, are more vulnerable to the disease. They are considered a high-risk group to the disease and require more resources in the course of outbreak management (Viboud et al., 2004). COVID-19 covers a variety of clinical manifestations including asymptomatic cases. Since the beginning of the COVID-19 pandemic, it has become apparent that the disease has particularly presented significant challenges and even fatal threats to more vulnerable individuals, including older adults with long-term medical conditions (Calcaterra et al., 2022). Literature reviews have also suggested the associations of increased risk of mental disorders between climate change, pollution, and COVID-19 (Chiu & Fong, 2022; Marazziti et al., 2021; Menculini et al., 2021). Therefore, the impact of COVID-19 on the mental health of older adults should not be overlooked and such pandemic, whether physical or mental, is a serious threat and obstacle to the achievement of sustainable healthy ageing. These issues pertaining to older adults have also led to significant concerns with due consideration of the continually growing worldwide ageing population (Chiu et al., 2022; Fong et al., 2021). In this chapter, the impacts of COVID-19 on the older adults living in nursing homes will be reviewed. The physical and mental health needs of older adults living in nursing homes will be further analysed and recommendations and strategic directions for the preparation of other large-scale epidemics or pandemics in the future will be suggested.

Challenges from the COVID-19 pandemic

The aged care services under COVID-19

The goal of a long-term care home is to ensure the day-to-day care of frail older adults. Most nursing homes are not equipped with the most advanced medical equipment. While these nursing homes are operated with a focus primarily on the provision of living rooms and general nursing services to residents, they are rarely equipped with isolation rooms. Therefore, when older residents have contracted the virus, they are more likely to require hospitalisation (Dadras et al., 2022). In addition, most nursing homes do not have a 24-hour doctor service, and they cannot meet the emergent needs of the older patients in terms of medical expertise. Therefore, residents with severe illness will be sent to the hospital for infection treatment and isolation measures (Szczerbińska, 2020).

Since older patients are more likely to develop severe clinical symptoms during their infection, long-term care homes have faced unprecedented challenges during the COVID-19 pandemic to maintain strict social-distancing measures (Noten et al., 2022). Nursing staff need to follow the guidelines of the Centers for Disease Control and Prevention to screen residents for confirmed cases every day, so as to detect them as early as possible and prevent the spread of the virus in nursing homes. Examples include those related to the measurement of body temperature, oxygen saturation, and typical symptoms such as cough and shortness of breath. Staff also need to conduct tests before going to work and avoid going to work when having symptoms to protect residents from infection brought into the facility by others (Szczerbińska, 2020).

Although each nursing home has slightly different restrictions, the vast majority of seniors were not allowed to leave the nursing home and had to stay in their rooms for activities or meals. Their access to other communal spaces, including play areas, eating areas, or outdoors, was prohibited, so seniors were not able to share meals or engage in face-to-face leisure activities with other residents. Also, no visitors were allowed to enter the facility. Only the medical staff and nursing staff who were allowed to work normally could deliver meals or provide nursing services (Noten et al., 2022).

Impacts of social isolation

Maintaining an appropriate social distance is recognised as an effective measure to reduce the spread of the coronavirus (Oliveira et al., 2022). Meanwhile, one of the major strategies of most countries to combat the virus was to stop all non-essential visits, leading to negative impacts of the lockdown on the older adults (Calcaterra et al., 2022). With regard to isolation, studies have shown that it would cause changes in the quality of life, health, and well-being of people, including healthy and active older adults, with significant negative effects on daily life. During the lockdown, which has led to social isolation and thus reduced social interaction and support, older adults experienced anxiety and depression, as well as reduced sleep quality, which undermined their sense of well-being (Colucci et al., 2022). Besides, the mental health of older adults living in long-term nursing homes has been affected by COVID-19. The reason is that various infection-control measures, severed social ties, and various changes in society and daily life have caused varying degrees of impact on the mental health of older adults. Due to reduced social engagement, residents may experience anxiety, cognitive decline, depression, and negative emotions (Bethell et al., 2021).

Furthermore, visitor bans have posed challenges to nursing homes, with residents prohibited from social contact. Communication was done through video calls, letters, window, or balcony visits. The time spent in contact with society was significantly reduced and became much shorter than before. Even for residents making frequent phone calls with relatives and friends, which may have reduced social contact barriers, the extensive circle of contact has been severely hampered, still causing residents to have negative emotional impacts, including feelings of loneliness and fear (Noten et al., 2022). Although nursing homes have professional medical staff to take care of the older adults, they cannot replace regular visits by familiar relatives or friends. Coupled with strict standard equipment requirements, including wearing of personal protective equipment such as masks and protective clothing, the pressure and feeling of strangeness experienced by the residents have been intensified.

On the other hand, social-distancing measures during the pandemic resulted in a sudden lack of physical activities and increased sedentary time. Reduced activity frequency and long-term sedentary conditions of older adults will lead to a significant decline in musculoskeletal strength, ultimately leading to increased risk of falls and serious trauma (Imaginário et al., 2021). Studies have also shown that older adults have poor self-awareness of health and may not be able to realise that their activity frequency has decreased, leading to the negative impacts of physical weakness including decreased muscle strength of the lower limbs, decreased muscular functions, and motor control ability (Oliveira et al., 2022). A nursing home with a comprehensive nursing team can provide nursing resources for older adults, including making beds for them and cleaning the room. Meanwhile, studies have shown that during the pandemic, seniors living in nursing homes could have a higher risk of falls due to factors such as restrictions on daily life, reduced physical ability, and medication (Imaginário et al., 2021). Such background would also amplify the risk of under-activity brought by social distancing and isolation interventions during the pandemic.

Impacts of COVID-19

Mental health

Several studies have reported that during the pandemic, the number of older adults suffering from depression and anxiety has been increasing (Kurniawidjaja et al., 2022). This was found to be associated with the implementation of precautionary measures including quarantines, social distancing, and travel restrictions. In particular, older adults would carry out social isolation in a very strict manner due to their high vulnerability. This situation was complicated by the fact that the older adults living in nursing homes had not met with their family members for a long time, further impacting their mood and sleep quality (Pascut et al., 2022).

Moreover, most of the activities of the older adults living in nursing homes are designated to observe the social-distancing measures which have imposed restrictions on eating and bathing. This protected mode of living limited opportunities for communication, group chats, or sharing among residents, exacerbating their risk of depression. They live in groups and could not eat, move together, or gather in the dining room. Instead of eating in the dining room, meals were delivered by nursing staff. This change of living style has reduced resident independence and closeness to other relatives and friends, affecting their mental health and well-being. Studies have shown that it can lead to increased risks of decline in cognitive function, memory, perceptual speed, and visuospatial ability (Colucci et al., 2022). In the case of prolonged isolation, older adults had lower chances to interact with other people, and the rapid change due to social-distancing measures had created a higher level of anxiety among them, due to their lower ability in handling new information. The situation would become worse for older adults suffering from other diseases that have suppressed their immunity, worrying that being infected with the COVID-19 disease would easily lead to their death (Pascut et al., 2022). The older adults, as a disadvantaged group, are more likely to suffer from depression. The reasons for the higher proportion of depression are not only related to physical and mental decline, but also to the higher level of dependence in daily life (Kurniawidjaja et al., 2022).

There were also studies reporting the association of lack of social support with depression among the older adults (Kurniawidjaja et al., 2022). It was found that the quality of life of the older adults who often stay at home or care institutions is worse than that of those who often go out. The results have further supported that adequate social life and engagement is important to maintain a good quality of life. Social isolation is also reported to be associated with other negative psychological effects on older adults, such as loneliness and feeling of lack of medical support. Furthermore, after prolonged social isolation, some older adults may lose the motivation to expand or re-contact their social circle, leaving them unable to continue to integrate into community life (Pascut et al., 2022). Also, social restriction measures may increase the psychological burden of older adults, reduce social contact, and lead to excessively cluttered information. Therefore, older adults are more prone to depression, anxiety, and emotional instability. Even when the society is returning to normal after relaxation of the social-distancing measures, many older adults may remain very stressed about the risk of contracting the virus as it is harder for them to understand how the virus has become less dangerous after vaccination and the effect of herd immunity, for instance. Overall, the social-distancing restrictions during the pandemic can lead to negative psychological effects on older adults such as an increased sense of loneliness, isolation, and emptiness, which are likely to exert a long-lasting impact (Kurniawidjaja et al., 2022).

Physical health

COVID-19 is a virus that mainly affects the human respiratory system. Common symptoms of infection include fever, dry cough, and difficulty in breathing. Since the outbreak of COVID-19, the virus has spread rapidly and widely from person to person (Yuki et al., 2020). Atypical presentations include decreased mobility, unexplained tachycardia, decreased daily intake, and dysphagia. As reported in the literature studies, COVID-19 has significant impacts on vulnerable groups, including older adults with chronic medical conditions (Calcaterra et al., 2022). Compared with young patients, older adults have a weaker immune system and decreased ability to suppress infection. In addition, most older patients suffer from various chronic diseases at the same time, making them more susceptible to infection and the development of severe symptoms of COVID-19. According to the results of lung examination, the severity of pneumonia in older patients infected with COVID-19 is higher, including lung muscle atrophy and weakened gas clearance ability (Dadras et al., 2022). Meanwhile, a review study of epidemiological data reveals that higher mortality rates of COVID-19 among older populations have been observed globally in different countries such as China, the United States, and Italy (Yuki et al., 2020).

In short, the isolation and social-distancing measures have led to changes in daily life environment, presenting huge challenges to the older adults by affecting both human health and quality of life. Changes in daily life such as restricted activities and persistent stress from uncertainty can lead to possible indirect or secondary effects on older adults such as increased rates of illness and hospitalisation (Colucci et al., 2022). For older adults, regular exercise and social activities are crucial for maintaining their physical and mental well-being. However, during the COVID-19 pandemic, the number of social behaviours has dropped significantly. As a result, older adults have decreased physical activity levels, which may eventually lead to loss of muscle mass and strength, as well as an increased risk of falls (Oliveira et al., 2022). Furthermore, older people were among the main victims in the pandemic and were more vulnerable to COVID-19 due to conditions of multimorbidity. The pandemic has forced older adults to avoid any contact or face-to-face interactions with other people, and they usually stay at home for self-isolation. Some older people living alone may be isolated from outside information under this circumstance (Kojima et al., 2021). These also have negative impacts on their physical and psychological well-being.

Comparison of aged care services between Hong Kong and Asia-Pacific countries

Hong Kong

In Hong Kong, about 15% of people aged 80 years or above live in nursing homes, representing one of the highest proportions in the world. Nursing homes in Hong Kong are mainly designed with an open layout and are divided into floors. Generally, only ordinary screens and single beds are used to divide an independent space for each resident (Chow, 2020). Some families in Hong Kong rely on residential care homes for older adults to take care of their older members. Some families, worrying about the quality of care in residential care homes for older adults, were unable to hire foreign domestic workers to take care of their older members due to quarantine restrictions during the pandemic. They could only rely on the hospital services to care for their older family members (Auyeung et al., 2021).

Living in a dense environment added a higher risk of transmitting the virus through close contact (Viboud et al., 2004). Since older adults generally live in groups in private nursing homes in Hong Kong, the crowded living space makes it easier for the virus to spread through the air, increasing the risk of infection for residents or staff. Therefore, the first measure was to strictly prohibit all visitors from entering the nursing homes, and residents mainly used video calls to meet with their families. Even if the restrictions were relaxed in the later stage of the pandemic, visitors needed to be tested negative in advance and had to wear a surgical mask before visiting. In terms of measures, there were also restrictions on visiting time and number of visitors (Chow, 2020).

There were guidelines for nursing homes to follow for the prevention of COVID-19. For example, staff had to wear personal protective equipment during their duties. Residents were advised to wear surgical masks if permitted, and staff on the same floor or area had to avoid going to other floors or areas to avoid cross-infection. Also, unnecessary group activities were avoided. In terms of environment, partitions were also installed with the dining tables in nursing homes and different meal sessions were arranged as much as possible to avoid gatherings. Good ventilation was maintained while the environment was kept hygienic and clean by more frequent and thorough sanitisation. For residents suspected of being infected, having symptoms, or just discharged were to be isolated first (Auyeung et al., 2021).

Experience from Asia-Pacific countries

Overall, COVID-19 is a global pandemic with unprecedented community spread around the world (Xie & Chen, 2020). Similar situations and corresponding measures have also been observed in other Asia-Pacific countries in the battle against the disease outbreak. In Thailand, after experiencing the first wave of COVID-19, the government announced a nationwide emergency curfew to effectively control and prevent COVID-19. For the preventive measures in nursing homes for older adults, staff and older adults need to maintain a physical distance of at least one to two metres apart, take temperature records every day, wash their hands regularly, and wear surgical masks (Srifuengfung et al., 2021). Similarly, the Japanese government also declared a state of emergency at that time. Movie theatres and department stores were closed, and people were urged not to go out as much as possible. Likewise, in Singapore, different measures have been implemented nationally to mitigate and control the spread of COVID-19 virus, such as restrictions on visitors to healthcare institutions including nursing homes, prescreening of visitors, and a decrease in unnecessary patient transfer (Lum & Tambyah, 2020; Tan &

Seetharaman, 2020). Heightened vigilance and recommendations to mitigate the threat of COVID-19 in long-term care facilities have been well advocated and reported (Lai et al., 2020; Yen et al., 2020). The report by Yi et al. (2020) has shared the experience of community nursing services in Singapore during the pandemic in the support of older adults with chronic health conditions. Measures for pandemic preparedness were adopted, while team segregation, active screening, triage in advance of visits, and other precautionary measures were implemented to reduce the risk of contracting COVID-19.

It is important to note that salient considerations were taken for active management and control of pandemic in the Asian context, in view of the diversity among the Asian-Pacific countries in terms of social-cultural heritage, healthcare settings, impacts of health inequity, and availability of resources (Lim et al., 2020). In the future, more innovations in healthcare services should be investigated and developed in response to the rising demands for innovative approaches to deliver healthcare services in difficult times such as pandemic outbreaks. Establishment of resilient healthcare systems for older adults is central to sustainable healthy ageing. Holistic approaches such as systems thinking are expected to play a critical role in further development of sustainable health systems and the achievement of Sustainable Development Goal 3 (Chiu & Fong, 2023; Fong & Chiu, 2023). Furthermore, teleconsultation, virtual meetings, and integrated collaborations and partnerships are worth further investigation and development for ensuring accessibility of healthcare services and continuity of care in times of global emergency (Yi et al., 2020).

Principles and strategic directions

Social support

Due to social-distancing measures and restrictions, older adults usually stayed in their rooms all day and lived alone. The company of family and friends is one of the most important spiritual supports for older adults, which helps to cope with life pressure and avoid loneliness and social isolation. Therefore, even if care institutions are not open to the public, other channels and methods are required to allow older adults to maintain long-distance contact with relatives and friends, while helping the older adults to develop physically and mentally (Eriksson & Hjelm, 2022; Pascut et al., 2022).

Since the COVID-19 blockade has a negative impact on the quality of life and well-being of older adults, it is recommended that in clinical practice for older adults, they should be encouraged and advised to engage in independent physical activities such as walking to improve and develop a more positive awareness of health. Healthcare professionals and carers should closely monitor the medical, cognitive, and psychological status of older adults, and intervene when necessary to improve their quality of life and well-being (Colucci et al., 2022).

Human body functions and neurological sensations will decrease with age. In addition, most older people suffer from chronic diseases, decreased ability of body balance and muscle strength, side effects of drugs, and an increased risk of falls. Studies have pointed out that proper participation in sports by older adults can improve physical flexibility, increase self-confidence, and overcome mental health problems such as social isolation and fear. Therefore, it is recommended that older adults participate in more exercise programmes such as the Otago exercise programme, or more leisure activities to enhance their physical functions. It is noteworthy that long-time stay in the indoor environment due to isolation may gradually reduce their physical strength. During the pandemic, online Otago exercise programme training can satisfy the older adults who were exercising at home to the greatest extent, breaking through time and space constraints. Group training can also expand the social network of the older adults, which is more impetus than exercising alone (Yang et al., 2022).

Clinical improvement

Although there are still many factors affecting the risk of falls among the older adults living in nursing homes, it has been reported that exercise programmes have certain positive effects on the prevention of falls among the older adults, including effective training in balance and postural control (Yang et al., 2022). Installation of electronic devices such as a large screen is also recommended so that the older adults can better enjoy interactive live exercise classes. Telehealth services should be further investigated and developed to provide more communication channels between residents, family members, and caregivers.

Conclusion

Due to the COVID-19 pandemic, the physical activity of older adults in nursing homes has been limited. They can neither have a normal social life in the nursing home, nor live a normal life due to severe infection. Collaborative efforts are required between various professionals in the nursing homes such as nurses, physical therapists, nutritionists, and health assistants. In line with the pandemic situation, besides taking into account the due isolation measures, it is also necessary to focus on the actual needs of residents in both physical and mental domains. Exercise programmes should be continually implemented and social activities through the use of different channels are encouraged to maintain healthy lifestyles for the residents, promoting the health and cognitive function of residents, as well as improving their quality of life. Furthermore, salient considerations in the Asian context should be made for effective management and control during emergency situations such as pandemic outbreak, in view of the diversity among the Asian-Pacific countries in terms of social-cultural heritage, healthcare settings, impacts of health inequity, and availability of resources. Innovative approaches for resilient healthcare systems and advanced technologies for telehealth services, incorporated with comprehensive integrated partnerships and collaborations, should be further investigated and developed to ensure accessible healthcare services and continuity of care, which are essential for sustainable healthy ageing.

References

Auyeung, T. W., Chan, F. H., Chan, T., Kng, C. P., Lee, J. S., Luk, J. K., Mok, W. Y., Shum, C., & Wong, C. (2021). Covid-19 and older adults: Experience in Hong Kong. *Asian Journal of Gerontology and Geriatrics, 15*(2), 54–59. https://doi.org /10.12809/ajgg-2020-424-oa

Bethell, J., Aelick, K., Babineau, J., Bretzlaff, M., Edwards, C., Gibson, J.-L., Hewitt Colborne, D., Iaboni, A., Lender, D., Schon, D., & McGilton, K. S. (2021). Social connection in long-term care homes: A scoping review of published research on the mental health impacts and potential strategies during COVID-19. *Journal of the American Medical Directors Association, 22*(2). https://doi.org/10.1016/j.jamda .2020.11.025

Calcaterra, L., Cesari, M., & Lim, W. S. (2022). Long-term care facilities (LTCFs) during the COVID-19 pandemic—lessons from the Asian Approach: A narrative review. *Journal of the American Medical Directors Association, 23*(3), 399–404. https://doi.org/10.1016/j.jamda.2022.01.049

Chiu, W. K., & Fong, B. Y. F. (2022). Chemical pollution and healthy ageing: The prominent need for a cleaner environment. In V. T. S. Law & B. Y. F. Fong (Eds.), *Ageing with dignity in Hong Kong and Asia* (pp. 277–287). Springer. https://doi.org /10.1007/978-981-19-3061-4_19

Chiu, W. K., & Fong, B. Y. F. (2023). Sustainable development Goal 3. In *Healthcare, environmental, social and governance and sustainable development in healthcare* (pp. 33–45). Springer. https://doi.org/10.1007/978-981-99-1564-4_3

Chiu, W. K., Fong, B. Y. F., & Ho, W. Y. (2022). The importance of environmental sustainability for healthy ageing and the incorporation of systems thinking in education for a sustainable environment. *Asia Pacific Journal of Health Management, 17*(1), 84–89. https://doi.org/10.24083/apjhm.v17i1.1589

Chow, L. (2020). Care homes and Covid-19 in Hong Kong: How the lessons from SARS were used to good effect. *Age and Ageing, 50*(1), 21–24. https://doi.org/10 .1093/ageing/afaa234

Colucci, E., Nadeau, S., Higgins, J., Kehayia, E., Poldma, T., Saj, A., & de Guise, E. (2022). Covid-19 lockdowns' effects on the quality of life, perceived health and well-being of healthy elderly individuals: A longitudinal comparison of pre-lockdown and lockdown states of well-being. *Archives of Gerontology and Geriatrics, 99*, 104606. https://doi.org/10.1016/j.archger.2021.104606

Dadras, O., SeyedAlinaghi, S., Karimi, A., Shamsabadi, A., Qaderi, K., Ramezani, M., Mirghaderi, S. P., Mahdiabadi, S., Vahedi, F., Saeidi, S., Shojaei, A., Mehrtak, M., Azar, S. A., Mehraeen, E., & Voltarelli, F. A. (2022). Covid-19 mortality and its predictors in the elderly: A systematic review. *Health Science Reports, 5*(3), e657. https://doi.org/10.1002%2Fhsr2.657

Eriksson, E., & Hjelm, K. (2022). Relatives' perspectives on encounters and communication in nursing homes during the COVID-19 pandemic: A qualitative interview study. *BMC Geriatrics, 22*(1), 706. https://doi.org/10.1186/s12877-022-03364-1

Fong, B. Y. F., & Chiu, W. K. (2023). A systems approach to achieving health for all in the community. In B. Y. F. Fong & W. C. W. Wong (Eds.), *Gaps and actions in health improvement from Hong Kong and beyond* (pp. 41–54). Springer. https://doi.org/10.1007/978-981-99-4491-0_4

Fong, B. Y. F., Chiu, W. K., Chan, W. F. M., & Lam, T. Y. (2021). A review study of a green diet and healthy ageing. *International Journal of Environmental Research and Public Health, 18*(15), 8024. https://doi.org/10.3390/ijerph18158024

Imaginário, C., Martins, T., Araújo, F., Rocha, M., & Machado, P. P. (2021). Risk factors associated with falls among nursing home residents: A case-control study. *Portuguese Journal of Public Health, 39*(3), 120–130. https://doi.org/10.1159/000520491

Kojima, M., Satake, S., Osawa, A., & Arai, H. (2021). Management of frailty under COVID-19 pandemic in Japan. *Global Health & Medicine, 3*(4), 196–202. https://doi.org/10.35772/ghm.2020.01118

Kurniawidjaja, M., Susilowati, I. H., Erwandi, D., Kadir, A., Hasiholan, B. P., & Al Ghiffari, R. (2022). Identification of depression among elderly during COVID-19. *Journal of Primary Care and Community Health, 13.* https://doi.org/10.1177/21501319221085380

Lai, C. C., Wang, J. H., Ko, W. C., Yen, M. Y., Lu, M. C., Lee, C. M., & Hsueh, P. R. (2020). COVID-19 in long-term care facilities: An upcoming threat that cannot be ignored. *Journal of Microbiology, Immunology, and Infection, 53*(3), 444–446. https://doi.org/10.1016%2Fj.jmii.2020.04.008

Lim, W. S., Liang, C. K., Assantachai, P., Auyeung, T. W., Kang, L., Lee, W. J., ... Arai, H. (2020). COVID-19 and older people in Asia: Asian working group for Sarcopenia calls to action. *Geriatrics and Gerontology International, 20*(6), 547–558. https://doi.org/10.1111/ggi.13939

Lum, L. H. W., & Tambyah, P. A. (2020). Outbreak of COVID-19–an urgent need for good science to silence our fears? *Singapore Medical Journal, 61*(2), 55–57. https://doi.org/10.11622/smedj.2020018

Marazziti, D., Cianconi, P., Mucci, F., Foresi, L., Chiarantini, I., & Della Vecchia, A. (2021). Climate change, environment pollution, COVID-19 pandemic and mental health. *Science of the Total Environment, 773*, 145182. https://doi.org/10.1016/j.scitotenv.2021.145182

Menculini, G., Bernardini, F., Attademo, L., Balducci, P. M., Sciarma, T., Moretti, P., & Tortorella, A. (2021). The influence of the urban environment on mental health during the COVID-19 pandemic: Focus on air pollution and migration—A narrative review. *International Journal of Environmental Research and Public Health, 18*(8), 3920. https://doi.org/10.3390/ijerph18083920

Noten, S., Stoop, A., De Witte, J., Landeweer, E., Vinckers, F., Hovenga, N., van Boekel, L. C., & Luijkx, K. G. (2022). "Precious time together was taken away": Impact of Covid-19 restrictive measures on social needs and loneliness from the perspective of residents of nursing homes, close relatives, and volunteers. *International Journal of Environmental Research and Public Health, 19*(6), 3468. https://doi.org/10.3390/ijerph19063468

Oliveira, M. R., Sudati, I. P., Konzen, V. D., de Campos, A. C., Wibelinger, L. M., Correa, C., Miguel, F. M., Silva, R. N., & Borghi-Silva, A. (2022). Covid-19 and the impact on the physical activity level of elderly people: A systematic review. *Experimental Gerontology, 159,* 111675. https://doi.org/10.1016/j.exger.2021.111675

Pascut, S., Feruglio, S., Crescentini, C., & Matiz, A. (2022). Predictive factors of anxiety, depression, and health-related quality of life in community-dwelling and institutionalized elderly during the Covid-19 pandemic. *International Journal of Environmental Research and Public Health, 19*(17), 10913. https://doi.org/10.3390/ijerph191710913

Srifuengfung, M., Thana-udom, K., Ratta-apha, W., Chulakadabba, S., Sanguanpanich, N., & Viravan, N. (2021). Impact of the COVID-19 pandemic on older adults living in long-term care centers in Thailand, and risk factors for post-traumatic stress, depression, and anxiety. *Journal of Affective Disorders, 295,* 353–365. https://doi.org/10.1016/j.jad.2021.08.044

Szczerbińska, K. (2020). Could we have done better with Covid-19 in nursing homes? *European Geriatric Medicine, 11*(4), 639–643. https://doi.org/10.1007/s41999-020-00362-7

Tan, L. F., & Seetharaman, S. (2020). Preventing the spread of COVID-19 to nursing homes: Experience from a Singapore geriatric centre. *Journal of the American Geriatrics Society, 68*(5), 942. https://doi.org/10.1111/jgs.16447

Viboud, C., Boëlle, P.-Y., Cauchemez, S., Lavenu, A., Valleron, A.-J., Flahault, A., & Carrat, F. (2004). Risk factors of influenza transmission in households. *International Congress Series, 1263,* 291–294. https://doi.org/10.1016/j.ics.2004.01.013

Xie, M., & Chen, Q. (2020). Insight into 2019 novel coronavirus—An updated interim review and lessons from SARS-CoV and MERS-CoV. *International Journal of Infectious Diseases, 94,* 119–124. https://doi.org/10.1016/j.ijid.2020.03.071

Yang, Y., Wang, K., Liu, H., Qu, J., Wang, Y., Chen, P., Zhang, T., & Luo, J. (2022). The impact of Otago exercise Programme on the prevention of falls in older adult: A systematic review. *Frontiers in Public Health, 10,* 953593. https://doi.org/10.3389/fpubh.2022.953593

Yen, M. Y., Schwartz, J., King, C. C., Lee, C. M., & Hsueh, P. R. (2020). Recommendations for protecting against and mitigating the COVID-19 pandemic in long-term care facilities. *Journal of Microbiology, Immunology, and Infection, 53*(3), 447–453. https://doi.org/10.1016/j.jmii.2020.04.003

Yi, X., Jamil, N. A. B., Gaik, I. T. C., & Fee, L. S. (2020). Community nursing services during the COVID-19 pandemic: The Singapore experience. *British Journal of Community Nursing, 25*(8), 390–395. https://doi.org/10.12968/bjcn.2020.25.8.390

Yuki, K., Fujiogi, M., & Koutsogiannaki, S. (2020). Covid-19 pathophysiology: A review. *Clinical Immunology, 215,* 108427. https://doi.org/10.1016/j.clim.2020.108427

5 Review of healthy ageing policies and strategies in selected countries or regions

Yumi Y. T. Chan and Chor-Ming Lum

Abstract

Globally, people are living longer. Most countries worldwide are experiencing a rapid growth in the population aged 65 years or above. This has caused changes in age structure in the community, with more economically active populations becoming older. Moreover, the trends in ageing population and longer life expectancy lead to multiple questions and concerns for policymakers worldwide. Many countries have implemented healthy ageing-related policies and strategies to handle elderly issues properly. Effective ageing-related policies and strategies are significant to help older adults remain active and independent. To improve the quality of life of the older population, health promotion and prevention policies directed at the older population should be considered. A quality policy framework for healthy ageing could ensure the healthcare and social security systems would sustain large numbers of the older population in the community and balance the role of the family and the state among the ageing issues. It could increase public awareness about the major role that older adults play as they age in caring for others. This chapter will review the impact of COVID-19 on healthy ageing policies and strategies in selected countries or regions outside the Asia-Pacific region and recommend a policy framework to governments and politicians.

Introduction

Globally, the ageing population issue is the most significant challenge in both medical and social demographics. According to the World Health Organization (WHO), healthy ageing is the process of an individual growing older while maintaining physical health, mental health, and social well-being. It involves the process of functional ability development and maintenance which enables older adults' well-being (Fallon & Karlawish, 2019). Recently, the proportions of older adult population in Japan, Finland, and Italy are the highest. Among the country members of Organisation for Economic Co-operation and Development (OECD), South Korea is the fastest ageing country in Asia

DOI: 10.4324/9781003436881-5

while Greece, Poland, Portugal, Slovenia, and Spain are the fastest ageing countries in Europe. The non-OECD fastest ageing countries are China and Saudi Arabia in Asia and Brazil in America (Rudnicka et al., 2020). Since January 2020, the outbreak of coronavirus disease 2019 (COVID-19) has influenced daily life in Hong Kong. The older adults were categorised as a high-risk group for the coronavirus disease, and they were disproportionately affected by the pandemic. In Canada, Europe, and the United States, the COVID-19 pandemic has brought attention to the significant number of older adults' death because of the disease. The low inoculation rate of older adults and highly dense-paced vertical lifestyle in certain regions may raise the challenge of pandemic management in the older population (Das, 2022). The growing older population and COVID-19 pandemic increase the demand for services that provide care and support to older adults. This situation also raises concerns regarding the effectiveness of healthy ageing-related policies and strategies.

Key to healthy ageing-related policies and strategies in the community

Healthy ageing policies and strategies are important to the community. Healthy ageing encompasses various dimensions, including maintenance of good physical and mental health, as well as social well-being in the community. Effective healthy ageing-related policies and strategies could address the specific needs and challenges faced by older adults. It can enhance the overall well-being and quality of life for the older population (Feng et al., 2020; Ye et al., 2021). Ensuring the accessibility of older adults to affordable and quality healthcare services may reduce their barriers to healthcare services, such as financial problems and transportation issues. Therefore, the older population can access a comprehensive healthcare service that stratifies their unique needs, such as chronic disease management, preventive care, and geriatric care management (De Biasi et al., 2020; Yang et al., 2021). Successful healthy ageing policies and strategies include excellent prevention and health promotion for older adults. Examples include encouraging healthy lifestyles and promoting regular physical activity for older population, ensuring older adults' accessibility to healthy food choices, and raising their awareness regarding the significance of preventive healthcare screening and vaccinations (Yen et al., 2022). This may prevent diseases before they occur among older adults or may help detect diseases at an early stage. It contributes to the prevention of disease deterioration as well as reduction of the medical load and healthcare costs associated with treating age-related diseases and disabilities (Lette et al., 2017; Okamoto et al., 2023).

Moreover, effective healthy ageing-related policies and strategies may create economic benefits to society. Constructive healthy ageing policies promote opportunities for older populations to contribute their knowledge, skills, and experiences to society. These policies, promoting mutual understanding, respect, and collaboration between different age groups and the general public, recognise the importance of intergenerational relationships. The healthy ageing policies that maintain health, functional abilities, and productivity of older adults may support active and productive ageing. These policies not only allow the society to have a more engaged and experienced workforce from the older population, but also reduce older adults' dependency on social welfare systems and increase economic contributions from older population (Okamoto et al., 2023; Yen et al., 2022).

Impact of COVID-19 on healthy ageing-related policies and strategies in selected countries or regions

The COVID-19 pandemic has had significant impacts on healthy ageing-related policies and strategies in various countries or regions, especially in the Asia-Pacific region and Europe. The COVID-19 pandemic brings out some issues about healthcare services, such as reduced accessibility of healthcare service for the older population. To manage these situations, different regions in the world have implemented new healthy ageing-related policies and strategies and improved the existing policies and strategies, including increasing healthcare accessibility, boosting health promotion and disease prevention in the community, adjusting employment policies, promoting long-term care and support services, and raising awareness about healthy living strategies among the older population.

Healthcare and accessibility

During the COVID-19 pandemic, accessibility of older adults to healthcare services was disproportionally affected. The older population has a stronger demand for healthcare and medical services, as older adults with COVID-19 are more likely to have poor outcomes. The comorbidity rates of older adults to COVID-19 are higher, and they are more vulnerable to severe inflammation and are at higher risk of death (Dadras et al., 2022). Several regions introduced isolation and quarantine policies to people infected by COVID-19 and close contacts of infected people, including Asia and Europe. These approaches and policies increased the difficulties in healthcare and medical accessibility for the older population. For example, China had implemented a lockdown management approach to the community during the pandemic which increased complications for older adults to reach healthcare services (Yin et al., 2022). Italy was the first country hit by the COVID-19 pandemic in Europe. In 2020, a cross-sectional study conducted in Italy found that there was a reduction of healthcare and medical access among the older population. The study illustrated that there were 22.4%, 12.3%, 9.1%, 7.5%, and 6% of the older population with decreased general practitioner (GP) visits, outpatient visits, diagnostic examinations, emergency department (ED) access, and hospitalisations, respectively (Vigezzi et al., 2022).

To cope with the negative impacts of the COVID-19 pandemic on healthcare and accessibility in the older population, various regions have implemented different health policies and strategies. Numerous countries have introduced remote monitoring technologies to support healthcare services to deal with the problems of difficulty in access to healthcare services among the older population. During the pandemic, different types of telehealth applications were applied for the older population. Telehealth is a broad term that encompasses diverse healthcare services delivered remotely using telecommunications technology. It involves providing remote healthcare services through phone calls, video conferencing, or secure messaging. It improves convenience and expands access to healthcare for patients requiring various healthcare services, including medical consultations, diagnoses, treatment, monitoring, and education (Gajarawala & Pelkowski, 2021). In New York, there were remote evaluations of older adults by an ED provider using a telemedicine platform during the pandemic, including online follow-up visits and treatment related to COVID-19 as well as other chronic conditions (Haimi & Gesser-Edelsburg, 2022). A cross-sectional study also discovered that 21.5% of the older population in Italy had increased telephone contacts with the GP (Vigezzi et al., 2022). Apart from remote monitoring technologies, China has promoted a homecare services system to improve the accessibility of healthcare services for the older population. As China had implemented a lockdown management approach in the pandemic, it was inconvenient for the older adults to access healthcare services. According to a survey result about the utilisation of healthcare services in China, 52% of respondents responded that the utilisation of healthcare services was affected by the outbreak of the COVID-19 pandemic, specifically clinical testing and drug purchase (Wei et al., 2022). To solve these problems, China promoted a homecare services system for the older population, which is a network of healthcare professionals that deliver medical and personal care assistance to individuals in their own homes. During the pandemic, the healthcare professionals provided door-to-door healthcare to the older adults according to their unique needs, such as medical care, personal care, companionship, household tasks, and therapy (Yin et al., 2022). The remote monitoring technologies and homecare services systems can increase the accessibility of healthcare services, optimise the utility of community health resources, and reduce the medical burden of older adults as well as the healthcare system.

Health promotion and disease prevention

Older adults mainly die of three causes, including cardiovascular disease, cancer, and respiratory system diseases. Apart from these health issues, infectious diseases such as influenzas and pneumonia are significant causes of death in people of an older age group. COVID-19 was a key threat for older populations in cluster environments, such as nursing homes, rest homes, and healthcare facilities. Mortality rate is a significant outcome indication for monitoring the COVID-19 pandemic. The COVID-19 mortality rates are higher in older population compared to younger population. The Centers for Disease Control and Prevention has discussed that population aged 60 years or above accounted for at least 80% of total COVID-19 deaths (Wong et al., 2023; Yanez et al., 2020). During the pandemic, older adults with severe infection monopolised the beds in hospitals for a long period. They usually had poor recovery and remained weak after leaving the healthcare facilities. This led to a long-term poor overall health condition for the older adults and increased costs for the healthcare systems as well as the society. Health promotion and disease prevention are effective ways to reduce both morbidity rates and mortality rates of COVID-19 among the older population.

During the pandemic outbreak, many regions have initiated public health campaigns promoting preventive measures, including mask usage and hand hygiene. Apart from personal hygiene, real-time polymerase chain reaction (PCR) tests played a major role in diagnosing COVID-19 and rapid antigen tests (RATs) played an important role in detecting asymptomatic persons. Rapid diagnosis is crucial to control the spread of COVID-19. Although the sensitivity of RAT tests is lower, they do not need specialised equipment, are easy to use, rapid, and relatively inexpensive compared with real-time PCR test. Several RAT kits have received in vitro diagnostics emergency use authorisations from the United States Food and Drug Administration. RATs are considered valuable for reducing the spread of COVID-19 through the early detection of cases and making contact tracing easier. Hong Kong widely administered RAT kits along with the real-time PCR tests in the pandemic, which reduced the transmissibility of COVID-19 and lowered the case fatality rate (CFR) as it facilitated early detection of asymptomatic cases (Peña et al., 2021).

In addition, Hong Kong implemented the StayHomeSafe Scheme, which is an effective social-distancing, isolation, and restriction intervention strategy to control the pandemic (Du et al., 2022; Sims et al., 2022). China and South Korea also adopted isolation strategies and coupled them with close contact tracing. India and Japan carried out social distancing interventions (Wang et al., 2022). Although the isolation policies could reduce the spread of COVID-19, they brought certain disadvantages. Isolation policies affected individuals who rely on community resources and networks for assistance, especially impacting the social support for older adults. They resulted in delayed diagnosis or treatment of conditions other than COVID-19, such as chronic disease management and the detection of other health problems. Also, prolonged isolation may have negative effects on the mental health of older populations. It can increase loneliness feelings, anxiety, and depression. Moreover, isolation policies have led to significant economic impacts on many businesses, such as tourism, hospitality, retail, catering businesses, etc. These businesses have faced financial losses and closures. It also increased the unemployment rate and reduced economic activity, which came with financial hardships for individuals and communities (Amirudin et al., 2021).

Apart from isolation policies, vaccination strategies have been crucial in the global response to the COVID-19 pandemic. The governments of different regions have implemented various vaccination approaches to ensure efficient and equitable distribution of vaccines. Many regions had encouraged vaccination of older populations to reduce the number of severe COVID-19 infections among the older adults. There was poor vaccination coverage among older populations as they usually have insufficient awareness of vaccination. For instance, based on the statistics of Centre for Health Protection, more than 90% of older adults in Hong Kong who died in the fifth wave of COVID-19 outbreak did not receive two doses of vaccines. This shows that low inoculation rates among the older population can contribute to higher fatality rates (Das, 2022). There was not enough publicity about COVID-19 vaccines as well as general routine vaccines among the older population. Besides, in general, vaccines were self-paid for older adults. These caused lower awareness and poorer coverage of vaccination among on the older population. China implemented a targeted vaccination strategy, prioritising high-risk groups, including older populations and essential workers. China used a variety of locations for free vaccinations, such as mobile vaccination units, community health facilities, and hospitals to facilitate and encourage vaccination among the older population. Additionally, China also developed a health code system that incorporated vaccination information to facilitate travel and access to public spaces (Sun & Wang, 2022; Zang et al., 2022). In early 2019, Europe introduced a holistic research project called VITAL (Vaccines and InfecTious diseases in the Ageing popuLation) to control infectious diseases in older populations (Van Baarle et al., 2020).

An effective policy framework for the world

During the COVID-19 pandemic, different countries and regions had implemented various approaches or strategies to cope with the virus, including 'net-zero COVID' policy, 'Dynamic COVID-zero' strategy, and 'living with COVID' strategies. As of that time, the COVID-19 pandemic was still ongoing globally, with variations in the situation across different countries and regions. By the end of 2021, many countries had decided to coexist with the virus and were moving towards various 'living with COVID' strategies. In China, the zero-COVID-19 policy officially ended on 8 January 2023 (The Lancet Regional Health Editorial, 2023). The governments and healthcare systems of different regions and countries had put much effort into dealing with the spread of COVID-19 and controlling the pandemic at a higher level with lower cost and shorter time. It is significant to minimise the impact of the pandemic on the normal lives of people, society, and the economy (Das, 2022).

Health promotion to older adults is an effective way to reduce morbidity rates and mortality rates of certain infectious diseases among the older population. It also enables the older population to improve their health. It can start with encouraging personal hygiene, such as hand hygiene and usage of masks. It is also useful to encourage older adults to have regular check-ups and preventive measures, including vaccination, cancer screening, and other interventions suggested by healthcare professionals. The older population is recommended to make positive lifestyle choices, such as healthy food choices and regular exercise. Engaging in lifelong learning and intellectual stimulation allows the older adults to adapt to changes and challenges in the community. The government and other related institutions are suggested to enhance social support systems for the individuals who rely on community resources or networks for assistance, particularly for the older population. Furthermore, the government is recommended to expand healthcare coverage for the older adults, so that they are more willing and able to access healthcare services. When necessary, use of technology for case management and contact tracing, and implementation of strict border controls and travel restrictions are effective for infectious disease management (Davodi et al., 2023; Fulmer et al., 2021).

References

Amirudin, A., Urbański, M., Saputra, J., Johansyah, M. D., Latip, L., Tarmizi, A., & Afrizal, T. (2021). The impact of the Covid-19 self-isolation policy on the occupations of vulnerable groups. *International Journal of Environmental Research and Public Health, 18*(12), 6452.

Dadras, O., SeyedAlinaghi, S., Karimi, A., Shamsabadi, A., Qaderi, K., Ramezani, M., Mirghaderi, S. P., Mahdiabadi, S., Vahedi, F., & Saeidi, S. (2022). COVID-19 mortality and its predictors in the elderly: A systematic review. *Health Science Reports, 5*(3), e657.

Das, M. (2022). COVID-19 and the elderlies: How safe are Hong Kong's care homes? *Frontiers in Public Health, 10*, 883472.

Davodi, S. R., Zendehtalab, H., Zare, M., & Vashani, H. B. (2023). Effect of health promotion interventions in active aging in the elderly: A randomized controlled trial. *International Journal of Community Based Nursing and Midwifery, 11*(1), 34.

De Biasi, A., Wolfe, M., Carmody, J., Fulmer, T., & Auerbach, J. (2020). Creating an age-friendly public health system. *Innovation in Aging, 4*(1), igz044.

Du, Z., Tian, L., & Jin, D.-Y. (2022). Understanding the impact of rapid antigen tests on SARS-CoV-2 transmission in the fifth wave of COVID-19 in Hong Kong in early 2022. *Emerging Microbes and Infections, 11*(1), 1394–1401.

Fallon, C. K., & Karlawish, J. (2019). Is the WHO definition of health aging well? Frameworks for "Health" after three score and ten. In (Vol. 109, pp. 1104–1106). American Public Health Association.

Feng, Z., Glinskaya, E., Chen, H., Gong, S., Qiu, Y., Xu, J., & Yip, W. (2020). Long-term care system for older adults in China: Policy landscape, challenges, and future prospects. *The Lancet, 396*(10259), 1362–1372.

Fulmer, T., Reuben, D. B., Auerbach, J., Fick, D. M., Galambos, C., & Johnson, K. S. (2021). Actualizing better health and health care for older adults: Commentary describes six vital directions to improve the care and quality of life for all older Americans. *Health Affairs, 40*(2), 219–225.

Gajarawala, S. N., & Pelkowski, J. N. (2021). Telehealth benefits and barriers. *The Journal for Nurse Practitioners, 17*(2), 218–221.

Haimi, M., & Gesser-Edelsburg, A. (2022). Application and implementation of telehealth services designed for the elderly population during the COVID-19 pandemic: A systematic review. *Health Informatics Journal, 28*(1). https://doi.org/10.1177/14604582221075561

Lette, M., Stoop, A., Lemmens, L. C., Buist, Y., Baan, C. A., & De Bruin, S. R. (2017). Improving early detection initiatives: A qualitative study exploring perspectives of older people and professionals. *BMC Geriatrics, 17*(1), 1–13.

Okamoto, S., Sakamoto, H., Kamimura, K., Komamura, K., Kobayashi, E., & Liang, J. (2023). Economic effects of healthy ageing: Functional limitation, forgone wages, and medical and long-term care costs. *Health Economics Review, 13*(1), 28.

Peña, M., Ampuero, M., Garcés, C., Gaggero, A., García, P., Velasquez, M. S., Luza, R., Alvarez, P., Paredes, F., & Acevedo, J. (2021). Performance of SARS-CoV-2 rapid antigen test compared with real-time RT-PCR in asymptomatic individuals. *International Journal of Infectious Diseases, 107*, 201–204.

Rudnicka, E., Napierała, P., Podfigurna, A., Męczekalski, B., Smolarczyk, R., & Grymowicz, M. (2020). The World Health Organization (WHO) approach to healthy ageing. *Maturitas, 139*, 6–11.

Sims, S., Harris, R., Hussein, S., Rafferty, A. M., Desai, A., Palmer, S., Brearley, S., Adams, R., Rees, L., & Fitzpatrick, J. M. (2022). Social distancing and isolation strategies to prevent and control the transmission of COVID-19 and other infectious diseases in care homes for older people: An international review. *International Journal of Environmental Research and Public Health, 19*(6), 3450.

Sun, Y., & Wang, W. Y. (2022). Governing with health code: Standardising China's data network systems during COVID-19. *Policy & Internet, 14*(3), 673–689.

The Lancet Regional Health Editorial. (2023). The end of zero-COVID-19 policy is not the end of COVID-19 for China. *The Lancet Regional Health: Western Pacific, 30*, 100702.

Van Baarle, D., Bollaerts, K., Del Giudice, G., Lockhart, S., Luxemburger, C., Postma, M. J., Timen, A., & Standaert, B. (2020). Preventing infectious diseases for healthy ageing: The VITAL public-private partnership project. *Vaccine, 38*(37), 5896–5904.

Vigezzi, G. P., Bertuccio, P., Amerio, A., Bosetti, C., Gori, D., Cavalieri d'Oro, L., Iacoviello, L., Stuckler, D., Zucchi, A., & Gallus, S. (2022). Older adults' access to care during the COVID-19 pandemic: Results from the Lockdown and LifeSTyles (LOST) in Lombardia project. *International Journal of Environmental Research and Public Health, 19*(18), 11271.

Wang, X., Shi, L., Zhang, Y., Chen, H., Jiao, J., Yang, M., & Sun, G. (2022). A comparative retrospective study of COVID-19 responses in four representative Asian countries. *Risk Management and Healthcare Policy*, 13–25.

Wei, X., Yuan, H., Sun, Y., Zhang, J., Wang, Q., Fu, Y., Wang, Q., Sun, L., & Yang, L. (2022). Health services utilization in China during the COVID-19 pandemic:

Results from a large-scale online survey. *International Journal of Environmental Research and Public Health, 19*(23), 15892.

Wong, M. K., Brooks, D. J., Ikejezie, J., Gacic-Dobo, M., Dumolard, L., Nedelec, Y., Steulet, C., Kassamali, Z., Acma, A., & Ajong, B. N. (2023). COVID-19 mortality and progress toward vaccinating older adults — World health organization, worldwide, 2020–2022. *Morbidity and Mortality Weekly Report, 72*(5), 113.

Yanez, N. D., Weiss, N. S., Romand, J.-A., & Treggiari, M. M. (2020). COVID-19 mortality risk for older men and women. *BMC Public Health, 20*(1), 1–7.

Yang, W., Wu, B., Tan, S. Y., Li, B., Lou, V. W., Chen, Z., Chen, X., Fletcher, J. R., Carrino, L., & Hu, B. (2021). Understanding health and social challenges for aging and long-term care in China. *Research on Aging, 43*(3–4), 127–135.

Ye, P., Jin, Y., Er, Y., Duan, L., Palagyi, A., Fang, L., Li, B., Ivers, R., Keay, L., & Tian, M. (2021). A scoping review of national policies for healthy ageing in mainland China from 2016 to 2020. *The Lancet Regional Health - Western Pacific, 12.*

Yen, D., Cohen, G., Wei, L., & Asaad, Y. (2022). Towards a framework of healthy aging practices. *Journal of Business Research, 142*, 176–187.

Yin, Q., Liu, X., Huang, C., Bi, W., Zhou, R., & Lv, R. (2022). Effect of COVID-19 on geriatric medical services in China. *Aging and Disease, 13*(1), 4.

Zang, S., Zhang, X., Qu, Z., Chen, X., & Hou, Z. (2022). Promote COVID-19 vaccination for older adults in China. *China CDC Weekly, 4*(37), 832.

6 Community model for sustainable healthy ageing

Wang-Kin Chiu and Ben Y. F. Fong

Abstract

It has been predicted that the global population of older adults will increase significantly from 901 million in 2015 to an approximate amount of 2.1 billion by the year 2050. While ageing is an inevitable and natural process, challenges presented by population ageing have led to growing interest in the study of healthy ageing, a multi-dimensional concept building on the three important health dimensions as identified by the World Health Organization (WHO): physical, mental, and social well-being. The importance of these health dimensions is also reflected by increasing studies investigating the critical issues in relation to the eight interconnected domains as proposed by the WHO Age-friendly Cities framework. In this chapter, research studies on determinants of healthy ageing, community gerontology, and multi-dimensional healthy ageing interventions will be reviewed. Meanwhile, the impact of social-economic and structural inequalities on healthy ageing should not be overlooked. Relevant studies comparing social-economic inequalities in healthy ageing will also be discussed. The findings, in connection with the pertaining issues cited in the preceding chapters of this monograph, are expected to provide insights and future directions for the development of comprehensive community-based programmes and models which aim at helping older adults to age healthily. The details will also contribute to perspectives and specific recommendations in relation to challenges of the COVID-19 pandemic and its impact on the individuals and society such as mental wellness and health equity. Moreover, the design and development of a community model for healthy ageing are critical components to the achievement of sustainable healthy ageing with reference to the Sustainable Development Goal (SDG) 3 proposed by the United Nations in 2015. The review findings presented in this work associated with the measurement and domains of healthy ageing will also provide important insights for future lines of research in connection with promoting healthy ageing during the post-pandemic era.

DOI: 10.4324/9781003436881-6

Introduction

The continually increasing life expectancy and declining fertility rates in many countries have contributed to a steady growth in the number and percentage of older adults around the world, leading to the worldwide phenomenon of population ageing (Fong et al., 2021; Ismail et al., 2021). It has been predicted that the global population of older adults will increase significantly from 901 million in 2015 to approximately 2.1 billion by the year 2050 (Seah et al., 2019). This fast-paced demographic transition has attracted significant interest from different stakeholders, and the importance of improving the lives of older adults has been emphasised by the United Nations General Assembly which declared 2021–2030 the decade of healthy ageing (Chen et al., 2022). With the rapid growth of older populations, the impacts and challenges of population ageing have aroused significant concerns. For example, the prevalence of chronic conditions among older adults and the escalating burdens of multimorbidity have led to surging studies investigating the correlations of chronic diseases (Chowdhury et al., 2023; Zhao et al., 2018), while more efforts are essential for the alleviation of disease burdens and alignment of healthcare services to meet the holistic needs of older patients. Meanwhile, older adults are vulnerable to the chemical contaminants in the environment, while the alarming level of chemical pollution has led to serious deterioration of environmental quality, posing significant challenges to their quality of life (Chiu & Fong, 2022; Simoni et al., 2015). Furthermore, population ageing can have profound impacts on societal and economic development. Previous studies have discussed the effects of population ageing on sustainable social security systems and economic growth and reported increasing recognition of the challenges presented by population ageing to the achievement of Sustainable Development Goals (SDGs) adopted by the United Nations (UN) in 2015 (Bai & Lei, 2020; Kudo et al., 2015). While ageing is an inevitable and natural process, the challenges presented by population ageing have led to growing interest in the study domain of healthy ageing, a multidimensional concept building on the three important health dimensions as identified by the World Health Organization (WHO): physical, mental, and social well-being (Lara et al., 2013). The importance of these health dimensions is also reflected by the increasing number of studies investigating the critical issues in relation to the eight interconnected domains as proposed by the WHO Age-friendly Cities framework (Lu et al., 2019).

   In this review study, research studies on determinants of healthy ageing, community gerontology, and multidimensional healthy ageing interventions will be reviewed. Meanwhile, the impacts of socioeconomic and structural inequalities on healthy ageing should not be overlooked. Relevant studies comparing socioeconomic inequalities in healthy ageing will also be discussed. The findings, in connection with the pertaining issues cited in the preceding chapters of this monograph, are expected to provide insights and future directions for the development of comprehensive community-based programmes and models which aim at helping older adults to age healthily. The details will also contribute to perspectives and specific recommendations in relation to challenges of the COVID-19 pandemic and its impacts on the individuals and society such as mental wellness and health equity. Moreover, the design and development of a community model for healthy ageing are critical components to the achievement of sustainable healthy ageing with reference to the SDG 3 proposed by the United Nations in 2015. With due consideration of the growing global population of older adults, the review findings presented in this work associated with the measurement and domains of healthy ageing will also provide important insights for future lines of research in connection with the promotion of healthy ageing during the post-pandemic era.

Determinants of healthy ageing

Healthy ageing is a multidimensional concept appertaining to all older adults, and the policy agenda of public health focussing on healthy ageing has become a top priority in many countries due to the continually growing demographic pressure resulting from the rapidly increasing older populations (Sowa et al., 2016). It is of paramount importance to investigate and identify the determinants of healthy ageing that are applicable across different communities. The need for comprehensive investigations has further intensified due to the COVID-19 pandemic which has significantly affected older adults, even those who previously had been in good health (Abud et al., 2022; Jowell et al., 2020).

Common terms adopted in ageing research studies include healthy ageing, successful ageing, and active ageing. However, while definitions of healthy ageing have been vastly studied and developed, consensual agreement on its content is still yet to be reached (Abud et al., 2022). This also presents a challenge for the planning and development of a comprehensive public health policy and community health model in the context of an ageing population. Rowe and Khan (1997) have given the classical definition of ageing in good health entailing the balance between three major components: absence of disease and related physical impairment, good functional capacity, and active social participation. This idea has put forward the importance of the inclusion of optimal social engagement and psychological well-being in the definition of ageing in good health. Several reviews in this research field have consolidated the internal and external factors promoting good health for older adults and enhancing their engagement in active and healthier lifestyles (Hornby-Turner et al., 2017; Menichetti et al., 2016; Sowa et al., 2016). A recent review by Lu et al. (2019) has identified that the term healthy ageing was most appropriate for their study, taking into account the definition by the World Health Organization (WHO), which suggests that health should be defined as a state of complete physical, mental, and social well-being. Obviously, being healthy is not merely determined by the absence of disease.

The definition by WHO has led to categorisation of healthy ageing into these important domains, facilitating the development of frameworks for assessing and guiding an individual towards healthy ageing. Recently, a number of studies have included determinants of healthy ageing within the three healthy ageing domains: physical, mental, and social well-being. For example, in 2014, Thanakwang et al. reported the scale and instrumental development for the measurement of the multidimensional attributes of healthy ageing among the Thai adults, with which an acceptable overall reliability and validity have been demonstrated. The reported scale, AAS-Thai, was culturally contextualised and considered as a promising tool for assessing healthy ageing levels within a Thai context in both community and clinical practice settings. While there have been considerable healthy ageing studies carried out among males in both healthcare institutions and communities, the experience of healthy ageing process by incarcerated older women is scarcely found. In 2018, Lucas et al. carried out investigations on the process by which imprisoned older women in the Philippines experienced healthy ageing. The Road to Success Model was developed to advance the understanding and knowledge of how imprisoned older women achieve healthy ageing. The study also led to the emergence of five phases in relation to healthy ageing, which are Struggling, Remotivating, Reforming, Reintegrating, and Sustaining. The findings provide important fundamentals and basis for further studies on the structural and procedural changes in prison, with the aim of achieving healthy ageing for incarcerated older adults.

Recently, Chen et al. (2020) have conducted a healthy ageing study on the old-old (aged 80 years or above) population group in Shanghai, which has increased steadily. Semi-structured and in-depth interviews were conducted with 97 old-old adults in the community, which have identified self-reliance as the goal of successful healthy ageing. The study has also identified four proactive behaviours: physical activity, financial security, community connectedness, and willing acceptance of reality. These four proactive behaviours were conceptualised in the study model and the findings have offered new understanding for maintaining self-reliance to achieve healthy ageing. Furthermore, in recent years, healthy ageing studies have also been carried out in many other regions around the world. Examples include Australia (Teh et al., 2020; Robleda & Pachana, 2019), Cananda (Wallack et al., 2016), Korea (Cha et al., 2012), and South Africa (Amosun & Harris, 2018). While the determinants may differ and vary due to factors such as geographical locations, culture, and gender (Löckenhoff et al., 2009), the insights gained from studies across regions are valuable to successful healthy ageing and development of sustainable health systems.

Among the reported studies, a considerable portion has investigated determinants within the physical domain, focussing on the necessity to maintain a good level of physical capability for achieving healthy ageing. For example, in the study by Wallack et al. (2016) which focused on 683 older adults suffering from multiple sclerosis, physical activity was addressed specifically as a subtype of 'lifestyle choices and habits' under the body category. Likewise, other studies have used diet as a determinant for physical well-being (Abud et al., 2022). For example, the study by Lucas et al. (2018) has proposed diet as an essential component of the sustaining phase of healthy ageing in view of its important role in supporting and maintain physical health.

Regarding the mental determinants of healthy ageing, four major categories have been identified: self-awareness, outlook, lifelong learning, and faith. Self-awareness includes self-esteem and self-achievement (Cha et al., 2012), resilience (Ploughman et al. 2012), body awareness, and a sense of purpose (Wallack et al., 2016). The determinant of outlook and attitude is closely related to self-awareness. The recent study by Amosun and Harris (2018) has reported the positive impact on ageing of having a good outlook and an optimistic attitude towards the future. Lifelong learning is found to have an intricate connection with the outlook or attitude determinant. The study by Thanakwang et al. (2014) has further emphasised the importance of engagement in active learning, particularly in the technology field, for the achievement of successful healthy ageing. Lastly, faith includes important aspects of beliefs, religion, and spirituality. It has been reported that ageing gives rise to challenges and difficulties for older adults to look forward to the future, while immersing themselves in faith leads to a higher sense of purpose in their lives (Robleda & Pachana, 2019).

Investigating social determinants of healthy ageing has also been a heated agenda in healthy ageing research, and relevant determinants have been extensively studied over the years (Abud et al., 2022; Marmot et al., 2012). Research studies have identified three major determinants in the social domain: social support, community engagement, and financial security (Baron et al., 2019; Menassa et al., 2023). Social support, referring to the building of relationships and rapport with both family members and acquaintances, has been reported as one of the most influential factors in various studies (Lucas et al., 2018; Robleda & Pachana, 2019; Wallack et al., 2016). Another identified determinant is termed community engagement, encompassing a wide spectrum of social activities ranging from voluntary services to religious gatherings. These activities give a sense of belonging and an enhanced acquittance with the community, and the positive impacts of engagement in community activities have been further supported in recent studies (Amosun & Harris, 2018; Teh et al., 2020). In addition, financial security is also an identified determinant of healthy ageing in the social domain. It was defined as being capable of maintaining a good quality of life (Robleda & Pachana, 2019).

Overall, the optimisation of various identified determinants is expected to result in healthy ageing. It is of paramount importance to establish a clear framework of factors influencing healthy ageing at an individual level, providing guidance to public service providers and policymakers for identifying and giving incentives to work towards health improvement and promotion, specifically focussing on particular determinants which are related to an individual's circumstances (Abud et al., 2022). In addition, investigations are worthwhile undertakings to better understand and integrate findings of older adults' health perceptions since their self-perceptions of health are critical predictors of survival and mortality (Song & Kong, 2015; Tan et al., 2014). It has been further suggested that policymakers should develop a comprehensive and in-depth understanding of the health perceptions by older adults for the planning and formulation of effective health policies which are centred at older adults. Meanwhile, it has also been recommended that health definitions should be evaluated and updated by healthcare professionals and service providers in accordance with older adults' health and ageing perceptions so that appropriate and efficient health interventions can be implemented (Song & Kong, 2015; Warmoth et al., 2016).

Community gerontology and healthy ageing interventions

Population ageing has led to extensive studies regarding determinants of healthy ageing. Its great challenges presented to many societies around the world, as well as profound impacts both on the individual and the life of the community, have further intensified the need of promoting strategies to achieve healthy ageing and the importance of designing and developing models of elderly care at the community level. Community gerontology represents a rapidly growing field of research studies aiming to develop effective strategies for implementing programmes which help the older adults to achieve the highest level of health and well-being in the context of social and community environments (Greenfield et al., 2019). In other words, it is referred to as an emerging area of research studies, investigations, policy, and interventions with an important objective to advance the understanding of social environments and communities in the foundational contexts of ageing and the associated diversity, for which this understanding will be leveraged for required changes towards healthy ageing (Mendoza-Núñez & Vivaldo-Martínez, 2019). In the study by Greenfield et al. (2019), a fundamental theoretical framework for community gerontology was presented with three major sections. The first part involved discussions of the meso-level as the unifying and fundamental construct for community gerontology. The second part described the focus of community gerontology on various pathways of mutual influence between the meso-level and increasing micro- and macro-contexts over time. In the final part, the emphasis of community gerontology was put forth on the participation of gerontologists in the various community change processes for the facilitation of better and more optimal ageing experiences among a diversity of population or community subgroups.

It is noteworthy that the participation of older adults is a key component in the development of gerontological programmes for strengthening the individual and social development of older adults in their daily environment. Health promotion programmes and empowerment activities are essential for the enhancement of resilience and improvement of reserve capacities to limitations with ageing spanning across different dimensions such as cognitive, physical, psychological, spiritual, social, demographic, economic, and cultural contexts (Mastropietro et al., 2021; Menassa et al., 2023; Nilsson et al., 2015; Wang et al., 2013). These activities, to a large extent, were basically framed in different ways across a variety of models. For example, the study by Mendoza-Núñez and Vivaldo-Martínez (2019) has focused on community gerontology with reference to a practical capacity-building framework. The framework was designed with the purpose of enhancing health promotion and engagement of older adults, which are important to achieve and maintain personal life satisfaction, physical, psychological, and social well-being. In addition, there were studies reporting the adoption of a health behaviour change approach for various important aspects in healthy ageing such as the achievement of self-efficacy and individual goals (Felix et al., 2014; Potempa et al., 2010).

Healthy ageing is considered a multidimensional concept associated with the worldwide growing population of older adults (Ng et al., 2009; Seah et al., 2019). While various multidimensional healthy ageing interventions have been designed to address physical, psychological, and social health among independent older adults in the community, it is also of imperative importance to review the intervention characteristics and effectiveness for identifying the complexity, patterns of variation, and methodological approaches in the development of a comprehensive and practical model for multidimensional healthy ageing interventions.

Over the recent decades, there have been reports investigating different multidimensional interventions for healthy ageing. Examples include preventive home visits which aimed at providing information on existing health and social services. They also addressed important themes such as ageing attitudes and beliefs, management of individual health, physical environment, socio-cultural interactions and commitment, as well as social-structural health (Behm et al., 2014; Gustafsson et al., 2013; Zidén et al., 2014). A recent study also reported the use of preventive home visits for identifying health concerns of older adults, as well as planning and evaluating nursing interventions through healthcare dialogue (Sherman et al., 2016).

In addition, there were increasing amounts of reported studies harnessing a variety of educational programmes for health promotion. For example, Escolar Chua and de Guzman (2014) have reported the adoption of an educational programme for the promotion of physical activity, mental simulation, social engagement, and new skill development. In 2012, Fernández-Ballesteros et al. implemented a university programme to promote knowledge and new technology for enhancing social participation and intergenerational relationships, as well as promoting individual development and well-being. Health education programmes consisting of physical and leisure activities were also developed for the promotion of physical activities and introduction of leisure activities to stimulate and enhance cognitive functions of older adults (Kamegaya et al., 2014). More recently, a self-care structured group programme was designed to facilitate the understanding of external life challenges confronting older adults through the sharing of information, as well as to review resources for improving the well-being of older adults (Tan et al., 2016). Furthermore, health assessment and education programmes were reported to demonstrate significant positive impacts on health behaviour. The identified behavioural changes include increased physical activities, higher consumption of vegetables, lower intake of alcohol and fat, increased intention of vaccination and health condition screening, and enhanced stress management (Johansson & Björklund, 2016; Kwon, 2015; Stuck et al., 2015). Overall, health education programmes have reported substantial improvements in quality of life and life satisfaction, and promotion of positive health behaviours. It has also been suggested that future studies regarding multidimensional healthy ageing interventions should incorporate more robust methodology and contextual information reports for the development of a stronger evidence base (Seah et al., 2019).

Sustainable healthy ageing model

Research studies to advance the understanding of determinants for healthy ageing and community gerontology are of continual importance to sustainable healthy ageing in view of the ever-growing population of older adults and the evolving societal circumstances. While community health is well-defined and key characteristics of a community health model have been proposed, the results of more extensive studies in the future will provide valuable insights which are expected to be complementary to the existing knowledge on community health model (Fong & Chiu, 2023). Meanwhile, to achieve sustainable healthy ageing, the current understanding of community health should be incorporated with the lessons learnt from unprecedented crisis and emergency situations such as the COVID-19 pandemic (Jowell et al., 2020). The pandemic has highlighted the interconnectedness of different systems with the health system and exposed the vulnerability of certain population groups, such as the older adults, to the pandemic impacts. More research studies on the adoption of systems thinking approaches, which have found promising applications during the pandemic, are necessary. They are important for the development of a sustainable healthcare system, which is an indispensable component for sustainable healthy ageing.

As discussed in the earlier section on community gerontology and healthy ageing interventions, research studies have reported that health education programmes have contributed to improved quality of life and promoted positive health behavioural changes. In addition, intergenerational service-learning programmes are important for health promotion to the older adults, while there have also been various reports of significant educational benefits to students for such programmes (Fong et al., 2023; Ruiz-Montero et al., 2020). It is noteworthy that the importance of educational programmes for healthy ageing does not merely come from health programmes specifically targeting older adults; education to the young generations also plays a critical role for its significance in moving the society towards a sustainable environment. A green and sustainable environment is essentially important for healthy ageing in view of the vast number of studies reporting the impacts of pollution on health and the high vulnerability of older adults to chemical contaminants (Chiu et al., 2022; Simoni et al., 2015). Growing reports have suggested positive impacts in the teaching and learning of environmental science supported by emerging digital technologies (Chiu, 2021). It is also noteworthy that while advanced technologies such as augmented reality and virtual reality have found promising applications in the enhancement of learning enthusiasm and promotion of active learning, reports have also demonstrated significant potentials for the applications of these technologies in environmental science education and training (Sermet & Demir, 2020; Wong et al., 2021). Further development of technological applications and incorporation of innovative approaches in education for sustainable environment are worth investigating with the goal of nurturing future leaders and scientists for a sustainable future. It is imperative that innovative modalities are not just designed for teaching specific knowledge and principles, but also for enhancing awareness of sustainable development and cultivation of responsible citizens. Moreover, the importance of environmental sustainability is also reflected by the SDG 3, with increasing studies reporting the connections between education and sustainable healthcare systems in the context of Environmental, Social and Governance (ESG) (Chiu & Fong, 2023a; Leung et al., 2023). Research studies investigating the incorporation of ESG in education are central to the attainment of a green and sustainable environment. More investigations in the future are needed for the achievement of these important goals.

Another critical issue to be addressed for sustainable healthy ageing is the remarkable differences in health status across and within countries in terms of life expectancy, health risk, disability, and incidence of disease at older ages (Hambleton et al., 2015). These differences constitute representative examples of health inequalities and present daunting challenges to sustainable healthy ageing. In recent years, there have been various studies investigating processes and policies to reduce health inequity for the promotion of healthy ageing (Östlin et al., 2011; Sadana et al., 2016). For example, studies regarding the implementation of universal health coverage have attracted considerable interests, aiming for the development of health policies and delivery of quality services which also extend coverage to all older adults without financial burdens (Goeppel et al., 2014; Sadana et al., 2016). These studies are also important for alignment with the indicative targets of SDG 3 and provision of further insights for attainment of healthy ageing in the post-pandemic era (Chiu & Fong, 2023b; Verguet et al., 2021). While there are various studies addressing health inequality and healthy ageing, it has been further suggested that priorities of research investigations should consider the strategic areas in alignment with a comprehensive model of sustainable healthy ageing. For continual efforts in the mitigation of accumulated inequalities, four strategic areas, namely underlying conditions and circumstances, integration across health and social systems, broader environmental context and mechanisms, and measurement of challenges and assessment of action impacts, have been specifically identified (Östlin et al., 2011; Winkler, 2013).

Conclusion

Studies regarding determinants of healthy ageing, community gerontology, and multidimensional healthy ageing interventions have been reviewed. With the significant global challenges arising from the growing worldwide populations of older adults, it is imperative for more extensive studies to formulate effective policies and community interventions for the promotion of healthy ageing. Based on the studies reviewed in this work, important components for a sustainable healthy ageing model have been discussed and identified. Overall, the key characteristics of a community health model (Fong & Chiu, 2023), including availability, acceptability, accessibility, affordability, achievability, comprehensiveness, continuity, co-ordination, client-orientation, and cross-discipline, are important components to be considered when designing interventions for achieving healthy ageing. It is also recommended that more research studies for advancement in the understanding of determinants for healthy ageing, implementation of interventions for sustainable healthcare systems, design of educational programmes for health promotion, facilitation of incorporating ESG in education for sustainable development, and mitigation of health inequalities, are urgently required for moving towards sustainable healthy ageing.

References

Abud, T., Kounidas, G., Martin, K. R., Werth, M., Cooper, K., & Myint, P. K. (2022). Determinants of healthy ageing: A systematic review of contemporary literature. *Aging: Clinical and Experimental Research, 34*(6), 1215–1223. https://doi.org/10.1007/s40520-021-02049-w

Amosun, S. L., & Harris, F. (2018). "What next now that you are sixty?"–Preliminary exploration of the self-reported aspirations of community-dwelling older persons in the Western Cape Province, South Africa within the active aging framework.

Physiotherapy Theory and Practice, 36(7), 791–798. https://doi.org/10.1080/09593985.2018.1508262

Bai, C., & Lei, X. (2020). New trends in population aging and challenges for China's sustainable development. *China Economic Journal, 13*(1), 3–23. https://doi.org/10.1080/17538963.2019.1700608

Baron, M., Riva, M., & Fletcher, C. (2019). The social determinants of healthy ageing in the Canadian Arctic. *International Journal of Circumpolar Health, 78*(1), 1630234. https://doi.org/10.1080/22423982.2019.1630234

Behm, L., Wilhelmson, K., Falk, K., Eklund, K., Zidén, L., & Dahlin-Ivanoff, S. (2014). Positive health outcomes following health-promoting and disease-preventive interventions for independent very old persons: Long-term results of the three-armed RCT Elderly Persons in the Risk Zone. *Archives of Gerontology and Geriatrics, 58*(3), 376–383. https://doi.org/10.1016/j.archger.2013.12.010

Cha, N. H., Ju Seo, E., & Sok, S. R. (2012). Factors influencing the successful aging of older Korean adults. *Contemporary Nurse, 41*(1), 78–87. https://doi.org/10.5172/conu.2012.41.1.78

Chen, L., Ye, M., & Kahana, E. (2020). A self-reliant umbrella: Defining successful aging among the old-old (80+) in Shanghai. *Journal of Applied Gerontology, 39*(3), 242–249. https://doi.org/10.1177/0733464819842500

Chen, X., Giles, J., Yao, Y., Yip, W., Meng, Q., Berkman, L., ... Zhao, Y. (2022). The path to healthy ageing in China: A Peking university–lancet commission. *Lancet, 400*(10367), 1967–2006. https://doi.org/10.1016/S0140-6736(22)01546-X

Chiu, W. K. (2021). Pedagogy of emerging technologies in chemical education during the era of digitalization and artificial intelligence: A systematic review. *Education Sciences, 11*(11), 709. https://doi.org/10.3390/educsci11110709

Chiu, W. K., & Fong, B. Y. F. (2022). Chemical pollution and healthy ageing: The prominent need for a cleaner environment. In V. T. S. Law & B. Y. F. Fong (Eds.), *Ageing with dignity in Hong Kong and Asia* (pp. 277–287). Springer. https://doi.org/10.1007/978-981-19-3061-4_19

Chiu, W. K., & Fong, B. Y. F. (2023a). Recent trends of research and education in ESG and sustainability. In *Environmental, social and governance and sustainable development in healthcare* (pp. 99–112). Springer. https://doi.org/10.1007/978-981-99-1564-4_7

Chiu, W. K., & Fong, B. Y. F. (2023b). Sustainable development Goal 3. In *Environmental, social and governance and sustainable development in healthcare* (pp. 33–45). Springer. https://doi.org/10.1007/978-981-99-1564-4_3

Chiu, W. K., Fong, B. Y. F., & Ho, W. Y. (2022). The importance of environmental sustainability for healthy ageing and the incorporation of systems thinking in education for a sustainable environment. *Asia Pacific Journal of Health Management, 17*(1), 84–89. https://doi.org/10.24083/apjhm.v17i1.1589

Chowdhury, S. R., Das, D. C., Sunna, T. C., Beyene, J., & Hossain, A. (2023). Global and regional prevalence of multimorbidity in the adult population in community settings: A systematic review and meta-analysis. *EClinicalmedicine, 57*, 101860. https://doi.org/10.1016/j.eclinm.2023.101860

Escolar Chua, R. L., & De Guzman, A. B. (2014). Effects of third age learning programs on the life satisfaction, self-esteem, and depression level among a select group of community dwelling Filipino elderly. *Educational Gerontology, 40*(2), 77–90. https://doi.org/10.1080/03601277.2012.701157

Felix, J. F., Voortman, T., Van Den Hooven, E. H., Sajjad, A., Leermakers, E. T., Tharner, A., ... Franco, O. H. (2014). Health in children: A conceptual framework for use in healthy ageing research. *Maturitas, 77*(1), 47–51. https://doi.org/10.1016 /j.maturitas.2013.09.011

Fernández-Ballesteros, R., Molina, M. Á., Schettini, R., & del Rey, Á. L. (2012). Promoting active aging through university programs for older adults. *GeroPsych, 25*(3), 145–154. https://doi.org/10.1024/1662-9647/a000064

Fong, B. Y. F., & Chiu, W. K. (2023). A systems approach to achieving health for all in the community. In B. Y. F. Fong & W. C. W. Wong (Eds.), *Gaps and actions in health improvement from Hong Kong and beyond* (pp. 41–54). Springer. https://doi .org/10.1007/978-981-99-4491-0_4

Fong, B. Y. F., Chiu, W. K., Chan, W. F. M., & Lam, T. Y. (2021). A review study of a green diet and healthy ageing. *International Journal of Environmental Research and Public Health, 18*(15), 8024. https://doi.org/10.3390/ijerph18158024

Fong, B. Y. F., Yee, H. H. L., Ng, T. K. C., & Chiu, W. K. (2023). Intergenerational service-learning: An experience in Health Promotion among undergraduate students in Hong Kong. *Journal of Intergenerational Relationships*, 1–14. https://doi.org/10 .1080/15350770.2023.2172514

Goeppel, C., Frenz, P., Tinnemann, P., & Grabenhenrich, L. (2014). Universal health coverage for elderly people with non-communicable diseases in low-income and middle-income countries: A cross-sectional analysis. *The Lancet, 384*(Suppl. 6). https://doi.org/10.1016/S0140-6736(14)61869-9

Greenfield, E. A., Black, K., Buffel, T., & Yeh, J. (2019). Community gerontology: A framework for research, policy, and practice on communities and aging. *Gerontologist, 59*(5), 803–810. https://doi.org/10.1093/geront/gny089

Gustafsson, S., Eklund, K., Wilhelmson, K., Edberg, A. K., Johansson, B., Kronlöf, G. H., ... Dahlin-Ivanoff, S. (2013). Long-term outcome for ADL following the health-promoting RCT—Elderly persons in the risk zone. *The Gerontologist, 53*(4), 654–663. https://doi.org/10.1093/geront/gns121

Hambleton, I. R., Howitt, C., Jeyaseelan, S., Murphy, M. M., Hennis, A. J., Wilks, R., & US Caribbean Alliance for Health Disparities Research Group (USCAHDR). (2015). Trends in longevity in the Americas: Disparities in life expectancy in women and men, 1965–2010. *PLoS One, 10*(6), e0129778. https://doi.org/10.1371/journal.pone.0129778

Hornby-Turner, Y. C., Peel, N. M., & Hubbard, R. E. (2017). Health assets in older age: A systematic review. *BMJ Open, 7*(5), e013226. https://doi.org/10.1136/bmjopen -2016-013226

Ismail, Z., Ahmad, W. I. W., Hamjah, S. H., & Astina, I. K. (2021). The impact of population ageing: A review. *Iranian Journal of Public Health, 50*(12), 2451. https://doi.org/10.18502/ijph.v50i12.7927

Johansson, A., & Björklund, A. (2016). The impact of occupational therapy and lifestyle interventions on older persons' health, well-being, and occupational adaptation: A mixed-design study. *Scandinavian Journal of Occupational Therapy, 23*(3), 207–219. https://doi.org/10.3109/11038128.2015.1093544

Jowell, A., Carstensen, L. L., & Barry, M. (2020). A life-course model for healthier ageing: Lessons learned during the COVID-19 pandemic. *The Lancet Healthy Longevity, 1*(1), e9–e10. https://doi.org/10.1016/S2666-7568(20)30008-8

Kamegaya, T., Araki, Y., Kigure, H., Long-Term-Care Prevention Team of Maebashi City, & Yamaguchi, H. (2014). Twelve-week physical and leisure activity programme improved cognitive function in community-dwelling elderly subjects: A randomized controlled trial. *Psychogeriatrics, 14*(1), 47–54. https://doi.org/10 .1111/psyg.12038

Kudo, S., Mutisya, E., & Nagao, M. (2015). Population aging: An emerging research agenda for sustainable development. *Social Sciences, 4*(4), 940–966. https://doi.org /10.3390/socsci4040940

Kwon, S. H. (2015). Wheel of wellness counseling in community dwelling, Korean elders: A randomized, controlled trial. *Journal of Korean Academy of Nursing, 45*(3), 459–468. https://doi.org/10.4040/jkan.2015.45.3.459

Lara, J., Godfrey, A., Evans, E., Heaven, B., Brown, L. J., Barron, E., ... Mathers, J. C. (2013). Towards measurement of the healthy ageing phenotype in lifestyle-based intervention studies. *Maturitas, 76*(2), 189–199. https://doi.org/10.1016/j.maturitas .2013.07.007

Leung, T. C. H., Chiu, W. K., You, C. S. X., & Fong, B. Y. F. (2023). Sustainable development in healthcare through an environmental, social and governance approach. In *Environmental, social and governance and sustainable development in healthcare* (pp. 1–9). Springer. https://doi.org/10.1007/978-981-99-1564-4_1

Löckenhoff, C. E., De Fruyt, F., Terracciano, A., McCrae, R. R., De Bolle, M., Costa, P. T., ... Yik, M. (2009). Perceptions of aging across 26 cultures and their culture-level associates. *Psychology and Aging, 24*(4), 941. https://psycnet.apa.org/doi/10 .1037/a0016901

Lu, W., Pikhart, H., & Sacker, A. (2019). Domains and measurements of healthy aging in epidemiological studies: A review. *The Gerontologist, 59*(4), e294–e310. https:// doi.org/10.1093/geront/gny029

Lucas, H. M., Lozano, C. J., Valdez, L. P., Manzarate, R., & Lumawag, F. A. J. (2018). A grounded theory of successful aging among select incarcerated older Filipino women. *Archives of Gerontology and Geriatrics, 77*, 96–102. https://doi.org/10 .1016/j.archger.2018.04.010

Marmot, M., Allen, J., Bell, R., Bloomer, E., & Goldblatt, P. (2012). WHO European review of social determinants of health and the health divide. *The Lancet, 380*(9846), 1011–1029. https://doi.org/10.1016/S0140-6736(12)61228-8

Mastropietro, A., Palumbo, F., Orte, S., Girolami, M., Furfari, F., Baronti, P., ... Rizzo, G. (2021). A multi-domain ontology on healthy ageing for the characterization of older adults status and behaviour. *Journal of Ambient Intelligence and Humanized Computing, 14*(7), 8725–8743. https://doi.org/10.1007/s12652-021-03627-6

Menassa, M., Stronks, K., Khatmi, F., Díaz, Z. M. R., Espinola, O. P., Gamba, M., ... Franco, O. H. (2023). Concepts and definitions of healthy ageing: A systematic review and synthesis of theoretical models. *EClinicalmedicine, 56*. https://doi.org /10.1016/j.eclinm.2022.101821

Mendoza-Núñez, V. M., & Vivaldo-Martínez, M. (2019). Community gerontology model for healthy aging developed in Mexico framed in resilience and generativity. *Journal of Cross-Cultural Gerontology, 34*(4), 439–459. https://doi.org/10.1007/ s10823-019-09385-5

Menichetti, J., Cipresso, P., Bussolin, D., & Graffigna, G. (2016). Engaging older people in healthy and active lifestyles: A systematic review. *Ageing and Society, 36*(10), 2036–2060. https://doi.org/10.1017/S0144686X15000781

Ng, T. P., Broekman, B. F., Niti, M., Gwee, X., & Kua, E. H. (2009). Determinants of successful aging using a multidimensional definition among Chinese elderly in

84   *Wang-Kin Chiu and Ben Y. F. Fong*

Singapore. *The American Journal of Geriatric Psychiatry, 17*(5), 407–416. https://doi.org/10.1097/JGP.0b013e31819a808e

Nilsson, H., Bülow, P. H., & Kazemi, A. (2015). Mindful sustainable aging: Advancing a comprehensive approach to the challenges and opportunities of old age. *Europe's Journal of Psychology, 11*(3), 494. https://doi.org/10.5964%2Fejop.v11i3.949

Östlin, P., Schrecker, T., Sadana, R., Bonnefoy, J., Gilson, L., Hertzman, C., ... Vaghri, Z. (2011). Priorities for research on equity and health: Towards an equity-focused health research agenda. *PLoS Medicine, 8*(11), e1001115. https://doi.org/10.1371/journal.pmed.1001115

Ploughman, M., Austin, M. W., Murdoch, M., Kearney, A., Fisk, J. D., Godwin, M., & Stefanelli, M. (2012). Factors influencing healthy aging with multiple sclerosis: A qualitative study. *Disability and Rehabilitation, 34*(1), 26–33. https://doi.org/10.3109/09638288.2011.585212

Potempa, K. M., Butterworth, S. W., Flaherty-Robb, M. K., & Gaynor, W. L. (2010). The healthy ageing model: Health behaviour change for older adults. *Collegian, 17*(2), 51–55. https://doi.org/10.1016/j.colegn.2010.04.008

Robleda, S., & Pachana, N. A. (2019). Quality of life in Australian adults aged 50 years and over: Data using the schedule for the evaluation of individual quality of life (SEIQOL-DW). *Clinical Gerontologist, 42*(1), 101–113. https://doi.org/10.1080/07317115.2017.1397829

Rowe, J. W., & Kahn, R. L. (1997). Successful aging. *Gerontologist, 37*(4), 433–440. https://doi.org/10.1093/geront/37.4.433

Ruiz-Montero, P. J., Chiva-Bartoll, O., Salvador-García, C., & González-García, C. (2020). Learning with older adults through intergenerational service learning in physical education teacher education. *Sustainability, 12*(3), 1127. https://doi.org/10.3390/su12031127

Sadana, R., Blas, E., Budhwani, S., Koller, T., & Paraje, G. (2016). Healthy ageing: Raising awareness of inequalities, determinants, and what could be done to improve health equity. *The Gerontologist, 56*(Suppl_2), S178–S193. https://doi.org/10.1093/geront/gnw034

Seah, B., Kowitlawakul, Y., Jiang, Y., Ang, E., Chokkanathan, S., & Wang, W. (2019). A review on healthy ageing interventions addressing physical, mental and social health of independent community-dwelling older adults. *Geriatric Nursing, 40*(1), 37–50. https://doi.org/10.1016/j.gerinurse.2018.06.002

Sermet, Y., & Demir, I. (2020). Virtual and augmented reality applications for environmental science education and training. In L. Daniela (Ed.), *New Perspectives on Virtual and Augmented Reality* (pp. 261–275). Routledge.

Sherman, H., Söderhielm-Blid, S., Forsberg, C., Karp, A., & Törnkvist, L. (2016). Effects of preventive home visits by district nurses on self-reported health of 75-year-olds. *Primary Health Care Research & Development, 17*(1), 56–71. https://doi.org/10.1017/S1463423614000565

Simoni, M., Baldacci, S., Maio, S., Cerrai, S., Sarno, G., & Viegi, G. (2015). Adverse effects of outdoor pollution in the elderly. *Journal of Thoracic Disease, 7*(1), 34. https://doi.org/10.3978/j.issn.2072-1439.2014.12.10

Song, M., & Kong, E. H. (2015). Older adults' definitions of health: A metasynthesis. *International Journal of Nursing Studies, 52*(6), 1097–1106. https://doi.org/10.1016/j.ijnurstu.2015.02.001

Sowa, A., Tobiasz-Adamczyk, B., Topór-Mądry, R., Poscia, A., & La Milia, D. I. (2016). Predictors of healthy ageing: Public health policy targets. *BMC Health Services Research, 16*(5), 289. https://doi.org/10.1186/s12913-016-1520-5

Stuck, A. E., Moser, A., Morf, U., Wirz, U., Wyser, J., Gillmann, G., ... Egger, M. (2015). Effect of health risk assessment and counselling on health behaviour and survival in older people: A pragmatic randomised trial. *PLoS Medicine, 12*(10), e1001889. https://doi.org/10.1371/journal.pmed.1001889

Tan, K. K., Chan, S. W. C., Wang, W., & Vehviläinen-Julkunen, K. (2016). A salutogenic program to enhance sense of coherence and quality of life for older people in the community: A feasibility randomized controlled trial and process evaluation*ucation and Counseling, 99(1)*, 108–116. https://doi.org/10.1016/j.pec .2015.08.003

Tan, K. K., Vehviläinen-Julkunen, K., & Chan, S. W. C. (2014). Integrative review: Salutogenesis and health in older people over 65 years old. *Journal of Advanced Nursing, 70*(3), 497–510. https://doi.org/10.1111/jan.12221

Teh, J. H. C., Brown, L. J., & Bryant, C. (2020). Perspectives on successful ageing: The views of Chinese older adults living in Australia on what it means to age well. *Australasian Journal on Ageing, 39*(1), e24–e31. https://doi.org/10.1111/ajag.12677

Thanakwang, K., Isaramalai, S. A., & Hatthakit, U. (2014). Development and psychometric testing of the active aging scale for Thai adults. *Clinical Interventions in Aging, 9*, 1211–1221. https://doi.org/10.2147/CIA.S66069

Verguet, S., Hailu, A., Eregata, G. T., Memirie, S. T., Johansson, K. A., & Norheim, O. F. (2021). Toward universal health coverage in the post-COVID-19 era. *Nature Medicine, 27*(3), 380–387. https://doi.org/10.1038/s41591-021-01268-y

Wallack, E. M., Wiseman, H. D., & Ploughman, M. (2016). Healthy aging from the perspectives of 683 older people with multiple sclerosis. *Multiple Sclerosis International, 2016*. https://doi.org/10.1155/2016/1845720

Wang, K. M., Chen, C. K., & Shie, A. J. (2013). GAM: A comprehensive successful ageing model. *Theoretical Issues in Ergonomics Science, 14*(3), 213–226. https:// doi.org/10.1080/1463922X.2011.617107

Warmoth, K., Tarrant, M., Abraham, C., & Lang, I. A. (2016). Older adults' perceptions of ageing and their health and functioning: A systematic review of observational studies. *Psychology, Health & Medicine, 21*(5), 531–550. https://doi.org/10.1080 /13548506.2015.1096946

Winkler, R. (2013). Segregated by age: Are we becoming more divided? *Population Research and Policy Review, 32*(5), 717–727. https://doi.org/10.1007/s11113-013 -9291-8

Wong, C. H., Tsang, K. C., & Chiu, W. K. (2021). Using augmented reality as a powerful and innovative technology to increase enthusiasm and enhance student learning in higher education chemistry courses. *Journal of Chemical Education, 98*(11), 3476–3485. https://doi.org/10.1021/acs.jchemed.0c01029

Zhao, C., Wong, L., Zhu, Q., & Yang, H. (2018). Prevalence and correlates of chronic diseases in an elderly population: A community-based survey in Haikou. *PLoS One, 13*(6), e0199006. https://doi.org/10.1371/journal.pone.0199006

Zidén, L., Häggblom-Kronlöf, G., Gustafsson, S., Lundin-Olsson, L., & Dahlin-Ivanoff, S. (2014). Physical function and fear of falling 2 years after the health-promoting randomized controlled trial: Elderly persons in the risk zone. *The Gerontologist, 54*(3), 387–397. https://doi.org/10.1093/geront/gnt078

Index